GUIDE TO WELSH WALES

First impression: October 1994

Cover photographs: Iolo ap Gwynn
All other photographs: Ralph Maud
Editing and design by Y Lolfa

ISBN: 0 86243 332 0

Printed and published in Wales
by Y Lolfa Cyf., Talybont, Ceredigion SY243 5HE;
ffôn (0970) 832 304, ffacs 832 782.

GUIDE
TO
WELSH
WALES

A week of day tours to the sites in Wales
most evocative of the national spirit
of the Welsh people

RALPH MAUD

CONTENTS

1.1 Offa's Dyke Centre, Knighton 1.2 Glyndŵr's Victory at Pilleth 1.3 Llywelyn's Grave at Abaty Cwm Hir 1.4 The Market Town of Rhayader 1.5 Llywernog Miners Trail

Preparatory Homework

2.1 The National Library of Wales 2.2 The Submerged Land of Cantre'r Gwaelod 2.3 The Contest of Traeth Maelgwyn 2.4 The Old Chapel Museum, Tre'r-ddôl 2.5 Taliesin's Grave 2.6 The Roman Road Sarn Helen 2.7 Y Lolfa Publishers 2.8 Glanfrêd and Edward Lhuyd (1660-1709) 2.9 Castell Gwallter at Llandre 2.10 Dafydd ap Gwilym's Birthplace, Brogynin 2.11 The Manor of Plas Gogerddan 2.12 The Church of Llanbadarn Fawr 2.13 The Grave of Lewis Morris (1701-1765) 2.14 The Hill-fort of Pen Dinas, Aberystwyth 2.15 Aberystwyth Castle

3.1 The Parliament House, Machynlleth 3.2 Dolwar Fach, Ann Griffiths's House 3.3 Glyndŵr's Birthplace,

FOREWORD

Although Wales, Cymru to the natives, is a small country, its prolific variety, its long history and rich culture, and its glorious landscape, combine to endow it with absorbing interest. In this enjoyable book, Professor Ralph Maud of Vancouver, who has long loved the land, writes of eight journeys, with Aberystwyth as their focal point, which cover a great part of the territory where Welsh was the language of the people from time immemorial. These tours provide a stimulating introduction not only to the country's enchanting beauty but also to its history and way of life, which throughout the centuries have been so different from those of its English neighbour. The book will enrich journeys made by car or public transport, but will also give the reader, whether a native or a visitor, great pleasure when read at home.

GWYNFOR EVANS

PREFACE

There is a Wales that the average visitor never sees, yet it is not invisible to Welsh people. The history of Wales as a nation is embodied in the old fortresses of the Welsh princes, the tracks that Owain Glyndŵr left on the landscape, the homesites and memorials of Welsh saints, preachers, politicians, and poets.

This guide proposes that to get the most out of a visit to Wales the reader must perform an act of historical imagination. You must put yourself, while you are here, in the place of someone looking east at an England which has been an alien intrusive force, whose attempted conquest never really succeeded, and whose influence on Wales will inevitably decline. I shall ask you to base yourself, literally and emotionally, deep in Welsh Wales, feeling the nostalgia of Welsh history and persistent beauty of the Welsh language. There are many unique Welsh characteristics that give assurance of nationhood to those who can claim it; and, made visible (which is the aim of this guidebook), they compel all right-minded people into a recognition of the logic of such claims.

I have chosen as our headquarters the place in Wales I know best and have been most fond of for thirty years. Because of its richness of history and its central position in Welsh Wales, Aberystwyth is an appropriate place to work from for day trips and to return to at night. It is an old seaside resort of ample and varied accommodation. (I would not want to be held responsible for disappointments, but I would hazard the opinion that it is not *necessary* to worry about booking in advance in Aberystwyth, one can expect such a range of hotels and B&Bs available at any time.) I am proposing a week of daily tours; but of course they can be spread out over two weeks on alternate days, and Aberystwyth, with its University, its National Library, and its resort events, will fill any 'spare' time.

So, as I write this preface overlooking Aberystwyth pier and the beach of Marine Terrace in a study kindly provided for me by the Extra-mural Department of the University College, whose director Professor Walford Davies has been a generous host to me on numerous occasions, I would like to thank him, and Hazel Davies, and my other Aberystwyth friends who have contributed to the making of this book. Above all others, Deulwyn Morgan will recognize how much of what follows is a result of our walks, drives, and supper conversations, which included Nans Morgan, and Lleucu, Rhodri, and Esyllt. It will become clear that the people of Llandre and environs have been a special resource: Tegwyn and Beti Jones, Lynn and Nest Davies, Elystan and Alwen Morgan, John and Eluned Rowlands, not to forget (how could one?) the late Mrs Towers. Cledwyn Vaughan stands out among the many who have helped me in the National Library. Old friends Meredydd Evans and Phyllis Kinney are joined now by newer friends John Harris and John and Helle Bairnie in giving me a sense of Aberystwyth as home, as the late Gwyn Williams and the now removed Ned Thomas used to do. I have made much use of Ned Thomas's *The Welsh Extremist* and Gwyn Williams's *The Land Remembers*. Meic Stephens has put us all in his debt for *The Oxford Companion to the Literature of Wales* and other source materials, as well as for his indomitable spirit. It is my privilege and pleasure to join the whole nation of Wales in paying tribute to Gwynfor Evans. The influence of his history of Wales, entitled in the English edition *Land of My Fathers* (now reprinted by Y Lolfa), can be discerned on every page of this guide; and I am able to devote one whole day ('Gwynfor's Country') to the parts of Wales that he has made most meaningful to us – and to me personally because of his generosity on several occasions in driving me to and fro in Dyfed. Beti Rhys of South Marine Terrace has accompanied me on several of the runs I have made along the proposed tour routes; her love of Wales has been infectious. Bruce Griffiths gave me a full day in Gwynedd, and Ioan Mai Evans in Llŷn. I could speak of many others in this regard, whose effect, though lasting, is less specific to these pages. They will recognize my silent thanks.

Finally, I thank the staff of Y Lolfa, and Robat Gruffudd who, since our first meeting in 1966, has been in my mind the inevitable publisher of this *Guide to Welsh Wales.*

Ralph Maud
Aberystwyth – Vancouver – Aberystwyth
1966-1994

The author at Taliesin's grave

Introduction

There are two sites that are of great importance to the author of this book, but they are too personal to be included anywhere except in this Introduction, where they can be used to contribute to an understanding of what it means to be Welsh. My vaguely discerned great-grandparents represent, like unknown soldiers, the battle for Wales.

My mother's grandfather, Henry Merton Jones, was raised in a thatched cottage in Llanstadwell, Pembroke. A photograph of this house, taken in the 1920s, would be the only remaining trace of him, except for the circumstance that during the month of January 1847 when he was born, the parish was visited in an official capacity by a Ralph Robert Wheeler Lingen. This was a man of 28, first class honours in Classics at Trinity College, Oxford, a Fellow of Balliol College, and about to be called to the Bar. He had been commissioned by the English Parliament, along with two others of his class, to investigate elementary education in Wales. In Llanstadwell he found no school at all, and wrote in his *Reports of the Commissioners* (1847) that 'in respect of educational resources, it may be said to be *magnas inter opes inops'* – that is, distinguished among the destitute. Bleak prospects for Henry Merton Jones.

But that is only half the story. The Welsh-speaking assistant with the Commission knew enough to visit Benjamin John and William Edwards at the Hephzibah Sunday School. Because it was a bitterly cold 10th of January, there were 'hardly any of the scholars present', but the implication is clearly that here was where the education of the young was carried out in Llanstadwell. This is one of the most important points to make about the nature of Welsh Wales: to a large extent it still exists as an entity because of the Sunday Schools. The Sunday School movement is described by Gwynfor Evans in *Land of My Fathers* as the most comprehensive educational system ever devised in Britain:

> It catered for all age groups and for all levels of intellectual ability. It provided motivation by awarding certificates and book prizes for good attendance as well as for attainment. Homework was set and syllabuses were prescribed. Written and oral examinations were arranged and periodicals sold through the Sunday Schools. In some areas even an efficient lending library service was included in this educational provision which affected whole communities . . . it was not unusual for more than 90% of households in Welsh-speaking areas to be associated with a Sunday School. The fruit of this work can be seen in the welcome given to a cart load of Testaments, of which an English traveller in 1810 has left this description:
>
>> 'the Welsh peasants went out in crowds to meet it and welcomed it as the Israelites did the ark of old; drew it into the town and eagerly bore off every copy as rapidly as they could be dispersed. The young people consumed the whole night reading it, and labourers carried it with them to the fields that they might enjoy it during the intervals of their labours.'
>
> In this way the life of the nation was transformed in the course of the nineteenth century.

The Commission of 1846-7 was totally blind to this kind of love of knowledge; its pig-headed description of a wasteland was rigged to justify the enforcement of English language and curriculum throughout Wales.

It is not without good reason that this Report has been called by Welsh leaders 'The Treachery of the Blue Books' ('Brad y Llyfrau Gleision'). The Commission's conclusions even ignored its own evidence. For instance, Henry Merton Jones's wife-to-be, Jane Williams, was about four years old when the Commissioners came to Llansamlet (then a village near Swansea, now a suburb) and visited her Infant school on 17 February 1847. 'Each scriptural lesson was illustrated by a scriptural print', says the Report in a rather approving tone. 'The master's manner was good and animated. The children appeared pretty well interested and attentive':

> He began by asking, 'Whom do we see in this print?' 'Jesus Christ.' 'Point him out.' They did so. 'What did Christ go about doing?' 'Curing.' 'What else?' 'Teaching.' 'How could we tell from this print that people like to hear Christ's teaching?' No answer. 'How can you tell a good preacher from a bad?' 'Because one preaches better than the other.' 'Suppose you were to find only three or four

people to hear the preacher at Cana (a neighbouring chapel),
would that be a sign of his being thought a good preacher or a bad
one?' 'A bad one.' 'How many are there to hear Christ preach in
the house?' 'It is quite full.'

The teacher went on to ask general questions, including the
distance of the sun from the Earth, which would have stumped
me. That 'almost all the answers came from the girls' I take to
redound to my great-grandmother's credit. But it should be
noted that the keenness was already being channelled away
from Wales: the children were being asked to repeat 'the
counties in England, locally grouped, as southern, midland,
etc.' So the Commission's conclusion that 'this school appeared
to be efficiently conducted' is double-edged. It is not
surprising that one of the consequences of this educational
process was that Jane Williams's daughter went to Yorkshire
as a nurse, married, and produced a line of Yorkshire born
men and women – even though some of them, like myself,
seem to spend a great deal of time in Wales. From this
personal perspective, then, this *Guide to Welsh Wales* can be
seen as an answer to those 'Blue Books', an attempt to repair
the torn pieces of my ancestry.

There is a third place, which seems to come out of a past
as distant as Llanstadwell and Llansamlet, so long is it since I
have been there. But the memory of Cesailgwm-bach is very
strong. This is a farmhouse located high in the hills above
Bont-ddu, near Dolgellau. Long given up as a working farm,
this cottage has for several decades provided a place in Wales
for Beryl and Peggy Jones, who, like my grandmother, left
South Wales and found work in Yorkshire. They were teachers
in my local school, and in my eighteenth year I was a guest at
Cesailgwm-bach, and learnt to love the walk along the
Mawddach estuary from Dolgellau to Bont-ddu that Ruskin
also though the most beautiful walk in the world. It is there
that I saw neighbouring farmers, who would not speak to each
other for the rest of the year, come together for sheep-shearing,
one to hold while the other clipped the struggling animal. The
Welsh ambience of Cesailgwm-bach, as well as the intense
literary discussions of its long evenings, these things are

formative in a life. And it was the place-name itself that opened up the Welsh language for me in an astounding way: *gwm* is the mutated *cwm* 'valley', and *bach*, as is well-known, means 'little'; *cesail* is in the dictionary as 'armpit', but Beryl and Peggy told me that was wrong, and gave me my first lesson in Welsh poetry. The people around there, they said, knew *cesail* as 'the place a baby's head rests when at the mother's breast'.

A NOTE ON MAPS & GUIDES

*This guide supposes that the reader will acquire a good map of Wales. The maps that the compiler has found most useful are, of course, the Ordnance Survey Landranger Series of Great Britain 1:50,000. Since it requires twenty-three of them to cover the whole of Wales, the average visitor will look for something else. Recommended is the Ordnance Survey Motoring Atlas 3 miles to 1 inch. The Wales Tourist Board Tourist Map 5 miles to 1 inch is good; so is the Leisure Map of Wales 1:250,000 (Estate Publications). My all-time favourite is the Hamlyn Leisure Atlas **Wales**, in hardcover book form, with Bartholomew maps of 1.6 miles to 1 inch, with a grid and easy to follow symbols on each page, and with ample notes at the back of the book. My copy is dated 1981; I have not seen a more recent update.*

*Of the more conventional guides to Wales, the Blue Guide's **Wales and the Marshes** (London: Ernest Benn; New York: Rand McNally) is fine. The recent **Mid Wales Companion** by Moira K.Stone (Anthony Nelson 1989) is commendable, as are the revised **Shell Guide to Wales** by Wynford Vaughan-Thomas, Peter Sager's **Wales** (Pallas Guides, translated from the German in 1991), and Siân Rees's A Guide to Ancient and Historic Wales (HMSO Cadw 1992).*

Some places this present guide proposes you visit may not be in any other guide or, in one or two cases, not even marked on the maps. Detailed instructions are therefore always given to make sure that destinations can be reached.

'The next best thing to a good guide
is an early start' – old Welsh saying.

Day 1

Across Offa's Dyke
o Aberystwyth

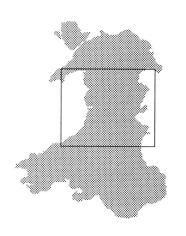

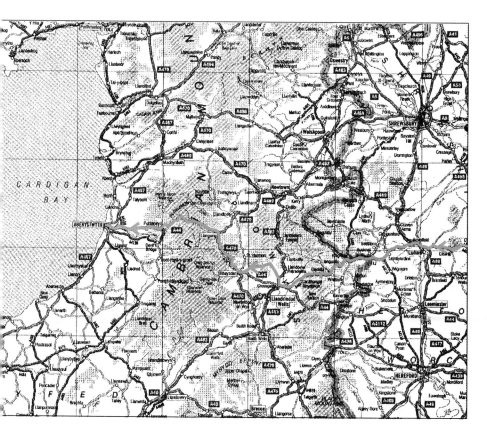

DAY 1: Across Offa's Dyke to Aberystwyth

The aim is to make an interesting entry into Wales, and reach 'base camp' at Aberystwyth in good time.

I	**From England on A4113 reaching border just before Knighton (1.1) and joining A488 (south).**
II	**From Knighton on A488 (south) – turn off left on B4356 to Pilleth (1.2).**
III	**Return to A488 (south, then west) joining A44 (towards Rhayader) – turn off right at Cross Gates on A483 then soon left on unnumbered road to Abbey-cwm-hir (1.3).**
IV	**From the Abbey continue west on the unnumbered road to reach A44 into Rhayader (1.4).**
V	**From Rhayader on A470 (north) joining A44 at Llangurig with optional stop at Llywernog Miners Trail (1.5).**
VI	**A44 terminates in Aberystwyth.**

I. A4113 from Ludlow is the entry of choice because Knighton gives us the best sense of that old symbolic border, Offa's Dyke. And there is the added symbolic fact that you reach the present-day border into Wales about 4 miles before the town and Offa's Dyke: Wales has gained 4 miles from ancient Mercia!

Once in Knighton, follow the signs for A488 (south, towards Llandrindod Wells), leaving the town centre on West Street, which is A488. There are signs to 'Offa's Dyke Centre', which is located on the right-hand side of the road in what looks like an old primary school (it was). Turn right into the car park to the left of the building, which is open 7 days a week 9-5.30.

1.1 Offa's Dyke Centre, Knighton

Knighton has been designated its new Welsh name on the basis of Offa's Dyke: Trefyclawdd ('Town of the Dyke') – abbreviated on some maps as Trefyclo. The dyke itself is signposted at the bottom of the field in front of you. You may find it a disappointment, for age and growth have blurred the distinctness of the earthworks. A pamphlet in the Offa's Dyke Heritage Centre will explain that it was never meant to be an effective military barrier, but represented a compact between Offa and the Welsh, agreed to by both parties to demarcate the newly established 'England' from the independent 'Cymru' (as the Welsh called their land – the word 'Wales' coming in around this time, the eighth century, from the Anglo-Saxon *wealas* 'foreigners'). It ran from Prestatyn on the north coast to Chepstow on the Severn River, and represented then, as it does now, the nationhood of Wales.

The visitor should be warned that the video show in the Heritage Centre gives little hint of this significance, dwelling almost entirely on the recreational aspects of the Offa's Dyke Path established in 1971 by the Countryside Commission of Parliament. It is a nice walk perhaps, but Offa's Dyke also represents twelve hundred years of separation. It is said that at certain times in the past a Welshman could have an ear cut off for being on the English side of the dyke. Today there is, I suggest, something of a reversal. The English visitor who crosses Offa's Dyke without due regard for the differences, will lose a great deal; it would be as though one's hearing was cut off.

> **II.   Though the consensus is that Offa's Dyke was largely an undefended border, we do know that the Welsh fought one strategic battle near here. We make now for Pilleth.**
>
> **From the Offa's Dyke parking lot, turn right on A488 and continue about four miles south to the first major turn-off to the right, B4356 (signposted to Presteigne). After about a mile, look out for a small white sign 'Pilleth Church' on the left-hand side of the road. The road sloping up to the left seems like a grass-grown track, but it takes cars up for a 3 pm service the last Sunday of each month. There is parking on a turn-about at the church.**

1.2 Glyndŵr's Victory at Pilleth

We have made this small detour to take cognizance of a Welsh military victory. I hate warfare, and it is not my intention to lead the reader from one battlefield to another. One of the gratifying side-effects of the Edwardian conquest is that Wales has not participated *as a nation* in any maiming and killing since 1283. However, the Battle of Pilleth counts as an extraordinary moment of exultation for the Welsh, and I see no reason to deny Welsh patriotism this one indulgence, and perhaps a few others.

It was St Alban's Day, 22

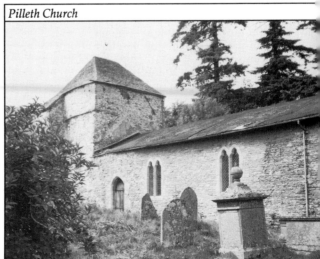

Pilleth Church

June 1402. After a century of English rule, a spark had lighted the tinder of discontent. Glyndŵr, chosen by his physique and character for a role of defiance, has taken up his fate. The English are unprepared for the skill and passion of the campaign, and Owain takes control of most of Wales (as we shall see in Day 3). His opponent at Pilleth was Edmund

Bryn Glas battlefield

Mortimer, now 25 years old, who rode out of Ludlow, recruiting local Hereford men, many of them Welsh, some of them Welsh enough to refuse to aim their arrows at Rhys ap Gethin, Owain's front-line captain. They turned them instead – or so it is reported – on Mortimer, who was forced to surrender.

This has been thought to have taken place on the hillside you can see behind Pilleth Church. 'Bryn Glas' is mentioned in despatches. But if Mortimer actually ordered an advance up such a steep incline he thoroughly deserves the disgrace of capture. And there certainly would not be much glory in it for the Welsh. More likely the battle took place on the flats by the River Lugg, as an alternative tradition records, and bodies were brought up to the church burial ground, to be discovered by a plowman five hundred years later, after the area had reverted to pasture. (The tall trees you see indicate where the mass grave was found.) This is the battle Shakespeare had a horrified courtier describe in *Henry IV Part I*:

> . . . the noble Mortimer,
> Leading the men of Hereford to fight
> Against the irregular and wild Glendower,
> Was by the rude hands of that Welshman taken;
> A thousand of his people butchered,
> Upon whose dead corpse there was such misuse,

Such beastly, shameless, transformation
By those Welsh women done, as may not be,
Without much shame, retold or spoken of.

This is typical atrocity propaganda. Thomas Thomas in his *Memoirs of Owen Glendower* (1822) offers a nice rebuttal: it was *after* these alleged barbarities on the part of Welsh women that Henry IV himself enacted legislation prohibiting any Englishman from marrying a Welsh woman. Who would have wanted to, asks Thomas Thomas, if the above story were true? Rather it was that Henry feared 'the charms of our countrywomen, whom nothing short of an act of the legislature could prevent his subjects from marrying.' We know as a fact that Edmund Mortimer, during his captivity, married one, Glyndŵr's daughter.

I can more easily believe the other charge: that the bodies of certain noblemen were not allowed from the battlefield 'without great sums of money being given.' That this demand was considered ungentlemanly only stresses how much this was a people's war. The participation of the *gwerin* (the workers of the countryside) meant it was more likely to be in deadly earnest. In any case, we should mark the words of Gwynfor Evans writing in *Land of My Fathers* about Pilleth:

> Some historians have referred to its barbarity. Hardly anyone today has the right to luxuriate in a feeling of superiority over the followers of Glyndŵr. Their wickedness was innocent enough compared with the horrors of Belsen and Siberia, Hamburg and Dresden, Hiroshima and Nagasaki, Viet-nam and Biafra.

The Church of Our Lady of Pilleth may be open, and one could do worse than pick up the pamphlet you will find there, and harken to its words:

> Before you leave this hallowed place, sit for a moment in silence and recall that for over a thousand years the grace of God in Word and Sacrament has been available here.

III. We now make for Rhayader and Aberystwyth, with one detour to Abbey-cwm-hir. We have to pick up an essential piece of Welsh history, the grave of Llywelyn the Last.

Return to A488 (west); drive a substantial distance to the A44 junction; turn right; but within two miles turn right again, at

1.3 Llywelyn's Grave at Abaty Cwm Hir

Abaty Cwm Hir (literally 'Abbey of Valley Long') was the second Cistercian abbey in Wales, founded in 1143. It was a show-place, only York, Winchester and Durham having longer naves. It was destroyed, yes, by Owain Glyndŵr, who thought the monks there had been acting as spies. It was rebuilt in part, but had only three monks at the Dissolution of 1536, when the whole was demolished down to the few ruins you can see.

We are here because of Llywelyn ap Gruffudd (1225-1282), referred to as 'Y Llyw Olaf' ('The Last Prince'), the last of the illustrious Welsh princes before the Edwardian conquest. He was killed at Cilmeri, and we shall have more to say about him when visiting the memorial stone there (8.2). His head was taken to London by royal decree for barbaric display; but his followers secured the headless body and brought it for burial here, the nearest abbey suitable for a prince's burial. This is the tradition, and there is no reason to doubt it. A modern gravestone has been laid flat to the ground where the chapel altar would have been.

IV. I am now proposing that you 'jump in the deep end' and drive one of the typical narrow roads of West Wales. Don't be frightened. You probably won't meet anyone. If a car approaches, the protocol is that, if you have just passed a suitable wide bit, you should back up into it to let the car pass. If you haven't, you wait and see if the other car has. If neither of you has, then there might be some discussion.

It is 5 miles of narrow road into Rhayader, joining A44 just at the outskirts. Proceed to the town centre (the clock). For a REST STOP, turn left on A470 (Builth Wells road) for about ¾ mile; be ready to turn left at the 'Bryn Afon Country House Hotel' and into a convenient parking lot. Bar meals are served in a pleasant informal setting, with some outdoor tables available.

At the crossroads in Rhayader there is a Tourist Information Office; and nearby, a small Folk Museum, free admission. To get the real ambience of this beautiful remote town, one must find the Falls themselves, from which the Welsh name of the town comes, Rhaeadr Gwy ('Waterfall of the Wye').

From the centre, follow the sign to Elan (B4518). Stop just over the bridge at the public toilets, or a few yards farther on at the car park of the sixteenth-century Triangle Inn or Tafarn Y Rhyd. Walk the few paces down the gradient to the quiet riverside park, Waun Capel Park.

1.4 The Market Town of Rhayader

This small market town has always been a stopping place for drovers, and now coaches. If it is Friday, you will see the lifestock market, or on Wednesday the general market. The town will reveal itself as the trading post for the farms around it; its history is the daily life of the common folk. As you look up at the hills from the riverside park, or as you resume your journey out of the town into instant moorland, you might ponder the words of the preacher and poet R.S.Thomas, who wrote the following passage when he held the living at Manafon about twenty miles north of Rhayader, words that were penned in 1945 but might still apply today:

> In these uplands we have a people who still enjoy life. Neighbour to the wind and cloud and the wild birds of the moor, they can still find time to 'stand and stare'. Let a man from the lowlands go up amongst them and they will keep him talking for hours, so ready are they to enjoy a little of the more sociable, human pleasures of life . . . Go up into these solitudes, and pass by one of these small farms with the scent of the peat coming sweetly to you from the blackened chimney, and likely as not the goodman of the house, if he sees you, will come towards you for the sake of a few words,

and after he has found out all about you with a disarming
ingenuousness, you will probably be invited to drink a cup of tea
with them in the kitchen. And on your departure you will meet a
stray group of dark-eyed children, the girls in red skirts, making
their way homeward from the distant school, that is often three
miles away . . . No one who knows this district intimately but can
feel its wayward and carefree charm, can but realise that here still,
however faintly, beats the old heart of Wales. That is why we are
all Welsh Nationalists deep down within us, even if we do not
subscribe outwardly to the policy of Y *Blaid.*

I ninnau boed byw	But give us to live
Yn ymyl gwisg Duw	At the bright hem of God
Yn y grug, yn y grug.	In the heather, in the heather.

> **V. Leave Rhayader on A470 to Llangurig, where the road to
> Aberystwyth takes the number A44. Drive carefully; this is a
> fast road, but has surprising curves. 'Perygl' is the Welsh word
> for 'danger'! Soon after the village of Ponterwyd there is on the
> right a well-marked tourist attraction for an optional visit.**

1.5 Llywernog Miners Trail

This was a working lead mine from about 1740 to 1914.
Restored in 1975 as an exhibition of one of the aspects of the
working life of this Welsh countryside, it is convenient to the
road, entertaining and educational. It closes at 5 pm, so the aim
should be to have been at the Welsh border at least by noon.

> **VI. A44 terminates in Aberystwyth at a rather awkward
> intersection with A487. First-time visitors might do worse than
> proceed directly across the intersection to North Road, drive
> along this distinguished residential street to its far end, making
> a left turn down to the sea front, then proceeding left along
> Marine Drive where parking and hotels are located. The Belle
> Vue Royal is a conspicuous landmark. The Tourist Information
> Office is just around the corner.**

Day 2

Welsh history around Aberystwyth

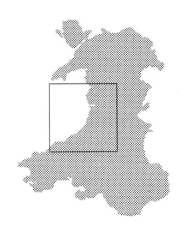

DAY 2: Welsh History Around Aberystwyth

PREPARATORY HOMEWORK

The following is an outline of historical periods as they relate to Wales.

(A) Prehistoric to 1000 BC

Populations followed the retreating glacial ice northwards, leaving traces in cave sites such as, in Wales, the famous Paviland Cave in Gower near Swansea. The later stone age people left primitive tools: archaeologists discovered a 'flint-chipping factory' for arrow and spear-heads near Aberystwyth harbour mouth. (Gerald Morgan has told me it is exactly on the spot where the Second World War concrete watchtower pillbox was erected, above the righthand side of the road to Tan-y-bwlch beach.) We will visit a local Neolithic burial site, Bedd Taliesin (2.5), and later (4.5) one of the finest examples of these slab-covered cairns at Bryn-celli-ddu in Ynys Môn (Anglesey).

Early Bronze Age settlers are sometimes called 'Beaker people' because of their grave urns. They may have been Celts of a type earlier than anything we could call 'Welsh'; but their many standing stones, round barrow burials, and stone circles everywhere in Wales indicate they liked this area. People have always liked Wales.

(B) Celtic period, about 1000 BC-50AD

There is an enormous number (about 580) of Celtic Iron Age hill-forts in Wales. Pen Dinas overlooking Aberystwyth is an impressive example (2.14). These corral communities were quite civilized and comfortable, and mainly continued intact throughout the Roman occupation. Druidism is the name for the religion and culture of these people. It might be useful to note that there were two separate waves of Celtic immigration: Goidel Celts settled Ireland, Scotland, and the Isle of Man; Brythonic Celts (hence the name Britain) settled Brittany, Cornwall, and Wales.

(C) Roman Wales, 60 AD-400 AD

The two big Roman camps in Wales were Caerleon in the south, and Segontium near Caernarfon in the north (4.2). We travel Roman roads more than once: for instance, Sarn Helen at Tal-y-bont (2.6), where there was also lead mining by the Romans.

A thousand Latin words came into the Welsh language at this time, including the common *pont* 'bridge', *melin* 'mill', and *mur* 'wall'. The Celts seemed to have absorbed from the occupying élite whatever was congenial to them. 'The impression which three centuries of Roman rule had made on the Welsh . . . became an integral and valuable part of the Welsh tradition; the spiritual and intellectual life of the people was leavened by Roman civility' (*Land of My Fathers*).

(D) Cunedda's Wales, about 400 AD-1066 AD

The Roman exodus was followed by invasions from Ireland; Cunedda is the one known to have led the resistance in Wales. He is thought to have been a Romanized mercenary from Manaw Gododdin near Edinburgh. Brythonic, he came back to save his fellow 'Britons' from Goidel domination. The Irish left their saints and a religious legacy symbolized by the Ogham (Goidelic) crosses at Nevern (7.6) and elsewhere.

Cunedda is said to have divided Wales among his eight sons: Meirion got Meironnydd, Ceredig got Ceredigion, etc. He established a royal house of long duration, of which the following is a much truncated tree of descent:

Cunedda (flourished 440 AD)
|
Maelgwn Gwynedd (died 547)
|
Cadwaladr ap Cadfan (defeated by Offa 634)
|
Rhodri Mawr (united Wales against the Norse, died 878)
|
Hywel Dda (established laws, died 950)
|
Gruffydd ap Llywelyn (1039-1063, killed by Harold before Hastings)

(E) The Welsh Princes, 1066 AD-1283 AD

William the Conqueror of 1066 fame established the Marcher Lordships of Chester, Shrewsbury and Hereford, and encouraged expansion westward through the building of motte-and-bailey castles such as Castell Gwallter (2.9). Norman attention to Wales in this period ebbed and flowed, as did the rivalries among the Welsh princes themselves. One to watch is Llywelyn ap Iorwerth, known as Llywelyn the Great, since he ruled all of North Wales in his time, married a daughter of King John, and obtained rights under Magna Carta. After his death in 1240, Wales relapsed into factions, until his grandson Llywelyn ap Gruffudd knitted together the pieces and refused homage to the new king Edward I. But he underestimated the determination of Edward, and independent Wales ended brutally in 1282-3. We have already seen Llywelyn's grave at Abaty Cwm Hir (1.3).

(F) Settlement; and Rebellion – 14th and 15th centuries

The uneasy peace after 1283 eventually made possible a flowering of Welsh poetry, notably Dafydd ap Gwilym (2.10). However, many felt keenly the insults of an occupation bureaucracy. Glyndŵr's War of Independence of 1400 (3.passim) was a moment of glory in this era of depression.

(G) The Tudors – 16th century

It is a paradox that the rise to the throne of Henry Tudor, a Welsh-speaking Welshman, proved to be very damaging to the independent spirit of Wales. His triumph at Bosworth Field in 1485 just meant that London drained the best minds of Wales into his service. His Act of Union 1536, which made Wales legally part of Britain, was not resisted.

(H) Inertia, and Resurgent Nationalism – 17th century to the present

Methodism vitalized Wales in the 18th century, but this religious movement was politically conservative. The Chartist radicals of the 19th century – despite the Rebecca Protests of 1843 – did not make serious inroads into the social fabric, until their descendants organized the Labour Party in the first years of the 20th century. Plaid Cymru ('The Party of Wales') is now the standard bearer in the fight for political autonomy for Wales.

DAY 2: Welsh History Around Aberystwyth

There is enough Welsh history within a ten mile radius of Aberystwyth to provide a fascinating day tour.

I	**From town centre on A487 towards Machynlleth – turn off right to the National Library (2.1)**
II	**Leave A487 left on B4572 to Llangorwen – stop for view above Borth (2.2)**
III	**Go through Borth, past Ynys-las on B4353 alongside Traeth Maelgwyn (2.3)**
IV	**Join A487 in Tre'r-ddôl – stop at the Old Chapel Museum (2.4)**
V	**Climb east from Tre'r-ddôl on unnumbered road, and turn right – stop at Bedd Taliesin (2.5)**
VI	**Proceed down to Tal-y-bont Church on possible Roman road Sarn Helen (2.6)**
VII	**Turn south on A487 – stop at Y Lolfa Publishers, Tal-y-bont (2.7)**
VIII	**Proceed south on A487, turning right towards Llandre on unnumbered road – stop at Glanfrêd (2.8)**
IX	**Turn right across railway at Llandre, climb past the church – enter field for Castell Gwallter (2.9)**
X	**From Llandre on B4353 to A487; left on A1459; left on unnumbered road to Penrhyn-coch – follow**

signs to Brogynin, birthplace of Dafydd ap Gwilym (2.10)

XI   Returning through Penrhyn-coch, stop just before A4159, turn right into Gogerddan (2.11)

XII   Cross A4159 over the hill to Llanbadarn Fawr – find the church off the main road (2.12, 2.13)

XIII South from Llanbadarn junction on A4120 to Southgate; right on A487 – turn off left at 'The Toll House' for climb up Pen Dinas (2.14)

XIV   Return to A487, and descend to Aberystwyth; turn left past the bridge to South Beach and Aberystwyth Castle (2.15)

Aberystwyth

I. The way this circle tour of historic sites is planned, there is little time to stop at any one spot. So, it may be best to save for later any investigation of the interior of the National Library. What we are mainly interested in is the significance of such an imposing edifice overlooking a town that shrinks in comparison.

Leave Aberystwyth centre on A487 (towards Machynlleth). Half-way up the first rise out of town, look for a sign on the right: National Library of Wales (or Llyfrgell Genedlaethol Cymru). Turn right into the driveway, and proceed to the car park. At least take in the building, and turn to look at the view of the town, one of the great views of Wales (or so it seems to scholars after a day's work inside).

2.1 The National Library of Wales

E.R.G.Salisbury of Chester, a well-known collector of Welsh and border books, wrote a letter dated 21 December 1873 to the *Carnarvon & Denbigh Herald*:

> Sir – the presence of Mr W.E.Gladstone at the Mold Eisteddfod, and the address which he delivered there, may, I hope, be regarded as an indication of a new era in the literary history of the Welsh people . . .

There was something afoot about a national library for Wales, but it was a decade before the 'Welsh Library' committee was formed under the chairmanship of Tom Ellis MP, and began co-opting members who were known to possess large libraries – including Lord Rendell, who had the foresight to buy and present to the committee the fourteen acres on which the Library was subsequently built. Cardiff's claim was strong, but a government decision in Aberystwyth's favour was made in 1905.

The first President of the National Library of Wales, Sir John Williams, the court physician, donated his private Celtic library as the foundation collection; and he ensured the National Library's greatness by persuading Mr Wynne of Peniarth to promise to the Library the Hengwrt and Peniarth manuscripts, so that it now owns the earliest extant manuscript in the Welsh tongue in the *Black Book of Carmarthen,* the earliest complete text of the *Mabinogi* in the *White Book of Rhydderch,* the earliest text of Hywel Dda's laws in the *Black Book of Chirk,* the unique *Book of Taliesin,* and many other rarities. Sir John officiated at the founding ceremony in 1911, but died in 1926, before the royal visit, which is commemorated by the carved stone of the outside stairs. A marble statue of Sir John at the west end of the Reading Room would not be sufficient in itself to coax one inside.

II. Return to A487, and continue up the hill. At the top, take the left fork, to Llangorwen (B4572). Past the village, with its distinctive churchspire, one sees on the left a signpost to Wallog, where Sarn Cynfelyn itself could be viewed, except that the road is 'Private'. Best to go on to Upper Borth for a most dramatic sense of the sea encroaching on the land. Be careful: there is no safe pull-out at the best view-point at the crest of the downward descent into Borth. Halfway down the hill there is parking for one vehicle and a seat at a good lookout point.

2.2 The Submerged Land of Cantre'r Gwaelod

One of the triads tells of the flooding of Cantre'r Gwaelod ('The Hundred Homesteads of the Bottom'):

> By this calamity sixteen fortified cities, the largest and finest that were in Wales, excepting only Caerleon upon Usk, were entirely destroyed, and Cardigan Bay occupies the spot where the fertile plains of the cantref had been the habitation and support of a flourishing population.

The way the story is usually told, a drunken watchman Seithenyn neglected the dykes. But Rachel Bromwich has a new translation of the crucial stanzas in the *Black Book of Carmarthen:*

> Stand forth, Seithenhin,
> and look upon the fury of the sea;
> it has covered Maes Gwyddneu.

Accursed be the maiden
who released it after the feast;
the fountain-cupbearer of the barren sea.

Who is this maiden? If the parallel situation in a Breton story cited by Rachel Bromwich is any guide, she is the scourge of God, punishing the land because of its wickedness. This idea of a Welsh Sodom may never oust the legend of the drunken Seithenyn; but perhaps it does not matter. The essential meaning lies elsewhere. Looking out over the Dyfi estuary and the shallow sand beach of Borth, you can see how the possibility of massive flooding might lurk continually in the psyche of the inhabitants. There may be a racial memory of such a happening. A submerged petrified forest reveals itself from time to time on Borth beach when the tide is very low. A Mr T.A.Morris once came across some curious bones projecting from the sand. They were those of an aurochs, the extinct precursor of the ox. There is some eerie sense of loss about this place, which gets itself translated into folklore. Some say that because of Seithenyn's carelessness ninety-nine towns were lost, the hundredth being Borth, the original name of which was Porth Wyddno ('The Gate of the City Under Wave'). Even today the spring tides regularly swirl through the ground floor of the houses on the sea side of the town, with or without a mythic Saturnius.

III.   There are bits of folklore every mile or so. There is no record of the actual Maelgwn Gwynedd's visiting this area, but there's a story about him, and a beach named Traeth Maelgwyn after him, though the name is slightly mis-spelled.

Descend into Borth, and drive along the main street (now B4353). Bear right with the road at Ynys-las; on your left are the marshes of Traeth Maelgwyn.

2.3 The Contest of Traeth Maelgwyn

A local story tells that Maelgwn Gwynedd 'the Ambitious' once called all the Welsh chiefs to Ynys-las to settle who would be supreme monarch of Wales. The chiefs were to sit on their thrones on the sand as the tide rose in the Dyfi estuary, and the man who remained longest in his seat was to be recognized as high king by all the rest. A henchman Maeldaf Hen constructed a throne of waxed bird's feathers, which floated Maelgwn Gwynedd on the water. When the rising tide toppled the others and compelled them to escape drowning, he was able to sit above the water in comfort. Ingenuity gave Maelgwn his desired supremacy, and the marsh was named after him. This 6th century story precedes the similar Canute story by five centuries.

> **IV. Proceed along B4353 up to the junction with A487, when you will see a service station. Cross the highway to it, and park in the lane behind it. Enter the gate at the sign to the Old Chapel Museum.**

2.4 The Old Chapel Museum, Tre'r-ddôl

Tre'r-ddôl means 'Village of the Meadow', and Humphrey R.Jones came to live here with his aunt in 1847 at the age of 15 when his parents emigrated to America. He began to preach; but, when unsuccessful as a candidate for the Wesleyan ministry, he emigrated too. He joined a revivalist sect in Wisconsin, and 'caught fire'. Returning to the Old Chapel here, he started the Welsh revival of 1858-1860.

The chapel is a museum now, but enough of the seating and the pulpit are left so that you may imagine Humphrey R.Jones towering above the audience –

> of robust athletic frame; his black hair thick, coarse, not very well arranged, dark, arched and heavy eyebrows, a ponderous, awkward bearing . . . He stands there very calm and quiet, but his face very expressive. He gives out a verse or two of a well-known hymn . . . First of all he speaks of the universal total depravity and sinfulness of men. *Tekel* is written on every heart. Solemnly he opens up man's lost and ruined condition and, as he does, the people draw nearer. Some rise from their seats. Some begin to weep. An old godly deacon, despised and hated for the truth's sake, rejoices to hear the old, loved truths set forth, and weeps

profusely. Then the revivalist begins to speak of the whole world as a graveyard . . . It was the old theology: the curse of a broken law; the substitutionary death of the Son of God, bearing the curse for the people; the complete removing of the curse, and every blessing flowing to sinners through the blood of Christ.

(The above is a description of Christmas Evans's famous sermon, but we can presume it might also apply to Humphrey R.Jones sixty years later in the The Old Chapel, Tre'r-ddôl.)

On growing into disuse, the chapel was bought and converted to a museum by R.J.Thomas, editor of the University of Wales Dictionary from 1938 to 1975. Downstairs are exhibition cases showing lead-mining, spinning, and peat-cutting equipment.

V. The next segment of the journey is a test of navigational skills, as you are asked to go straight up into the hills by a little-used road. The thing to remember is that you may think you are lost, but you will find, if you persist, that you are not.

Find the side road east from Tre'r-ddôl by going the few yards into the village and turning left just before the hump-bridge over Afon Cletwr. For a while this road is practically perpendicular. Turn right eventually at the junction on to a road that winds down into a ravine, where a bridge crosses the Afon Cletwr, and winds steeply up again. You may find you have to open and close a gate before the bridge and another some time after. Don't worry; this is a public road. After the farmhouse of Gwar-cwm, you will come out into a landscape of open fields, with a magnificent view of Borth and the lowlands you were recently driving through. Park immediately after a third gate (which may be open); you know you have arrived when you see in front of you in the middle distance an old farm with a new Nissan hut, and on your immediate left the beginning of moorland with its clumps of bracken. Climb up for a few yards: you will see a large stone propped on others, and the outline of a stone circle much disturbed by time.

2.5 Taliesin's Grave

As legend has it, the ex-king Gwyddno, in reduced circumstances after the flooding of Cantre'r Gwaelod (2.2), took to fishing in the estuary of the River Leri at Borth. The first of May was always a big catch, so he generously gave the weir over that day to his married son Elffin. But that year there

Taliesin's grave

were absolutely no fish at all – only a leather bag containing a baby boy. He had such a beautiful head that Elffin named him Taliesin ('brow lucent'). Elffin thought that this did not quite make up for his zero catch – until Taliesin in his saddlebag began precociously to sing *in regular bardic metres*. Taliesin grew up to be the greatest poet of all time, and we have *The Book of Taliesin* to prove it. And we have his grave (Bedd Taliesin) up above the Leri.

There was an actual poet of the sixth century called Taliesin; but of course he is not the miraculous boy of the legend, nor is Bedd Taliesin his grave. What you see here is one of many similar Bronze Age burial cairns of at least 3000 years ago, with the slab dislodged and the stones in disarray.

This unmade *bedd* was visited by the Cambrian Archaeological Society on 8 September 1847 in 'most favourable weather'. Three carriages of enthusiasts, including the Deans of Hereford and Bangor, set off after breakfast in the public rooms. They reported that the cairn was 135 ft in circumference, the central cist about 8 ft long by 2 ft 6 inches wide. The slab that formerly covered the grave was measured at 5 ft 9 inches. A 'most amusing incident' occurred when the

Dean of Hereford slipped at the brink of the grave and fell, ending prone in a full length posture. 'Thereupon the Dean of Bangor, sympathising with him, said he should not remain there alone, and immediately leaped in and took his station by the side of his brother dean to the intense delight of the spectators.' Looking at the site today, you may wonder how it had room in it for two full length deans. This may be just one more bit of mythology surrounding Bedd Taliesin!

> **VI.   At the farm, turn right through a final closed gate. Turn next left, and proceed south down what is a more well-used road, which has long been thought to be part of the network of Roman roads in Wales.**

2.6 The Roman Road Sarn Helen

Helen was the Celtic wife of Magnus Maximus, the Roman governor of Britain in the late fourth century. The idea of her being concerned with roads is nice, but the name 'Sarn Helen' is thought to come form *sarn* 'causeway' and *elin*, the Welsh word for 'elbow' or 'angle' – indicating that for West Wales the Roman roads had to abandon their normal straightness. It is therefore probably wrong to say that the road you have just travelled on is Roman, just because it's a straight line on a map. They didn't build the Roman empire with such pig-headedness. Indeed, there is recent evidence that the Romans actually followed the present A487 of today, which sensibly skirts the foothills below. An archaeologist J.L.Davies found the remains of a Roman camp at Erglodd (though nothing that can be seen today with the naked eye), just down the road from Tre'r-ddôl on the way we would have come if we had taken the easy route.

> **VII.   Bear right with the road on your descent down to A487 by Tal-y-bont Church. Turn left and proceed into the village, looking out for a sign 'Y Lolfa' on what looks like an old police**

station (it was) on the left-hand side of the road. Drop in and visit the Press, and the book display.

2.7 Y Lolfa Publishers

Y Lolfa ('The Lounge' – with almost untranslatable implications: 'The Fun Place') is a publishing venture started in Tal-y-bont in 1966 by a young nationalist Robat Gruffudd, who had just gained newspaper headlines by refusing to accept his degree from the University because the certificate was not in Welsh. An engaging personality, he singlehandedly took on the Welsh establishment, producing a satirical and bawdy

Y Lolfa

magazine *Lol*, read secretly by everybody at the National Eisteddfod each year. He has attempted to make Welsh language learning fun by a series of popular primers. He has published serious books on nationalist themes, both in Welsh and in English. And he has made a success of it, as you can see. He has taken over the old police station which, it is said, he used to visit previously in his role as protester.

REST STOP in Tal-y-bont: the choice of White or Black Lions, on the village green.

VIII. Continue south on A487 towards Aberystwyth, but turn on the first signposted road to the right, towards Llandre.

About ½ mile down this narrow hedged lane, there is an entrance on the right to 'Riverside Caravans'. Stopping at this point, you can see the old farmhouse (private) of Glanfrêd on the rise.

2.8 Glanfrêd and Edward Lhuyd (1660-1709)

Glanfrêd was the home of the mother of Edward Lhuyd, the great zoological taxologist, who, in a lifetime of assiduous work, transformed the Ashmolean Museum at Oxford. But Lhuyd did not stay at his desk; and, especially when he was asked to revise the 1695 edition of Camden's great encyclopaedia *Britannia*, he examined many sites in person, including one that we have just seen, which happened to be near his mother's home. The following note gives some indication of his seventeenth century scientific hauteur:

> Gwely Taliesin, in the parish of *Llan-Vihangel geneu'r glyn*, by its name and the tradition of the neighbours concerning it, ought to be the grave of the celebrated Poet *Taliesin ben beirdh*, who flourished about the year 540. This grave or bed (for that is the significance of the word *Gwely*) seems also to be a sort of *Kist-vaen*, four feet in length, and three in bredth, composed of four stones, one at each end, and two side-stones, the higher of which is about a foot above ground. I take this, and all others of this kind, to be old heathen Monuments, and am far from believing that *Taliesin* was inter'd here.

Edward Lhuyd would not find many such opportunities to visit his mother's house. We mention him here as further illustration of the premise that there is hardly a spot in this landscape that does not have some associations of interest. (Half a mile down the road from Glanfrêd is another house, Dolgwiail . . . where the present writer is often pleased to stay on visits to Wales!)

IX. The Glanfrêd road joins B4353 going south into the village of Llandre, previously Llanfihangel Genau'r-glyn ('St Michael's of the Opening of the Valley'), which name the church there still has. Turn right at the railway crossing, and proceed up the village, and bear right on the road that rises steeply behind the church. Take the very sharp turn left at the top of the rise, and stop at the first gate on the left. A pathway of sorts can be seen going across the field, which may be dampish, depending on the time of year. Anyone with proper footwear reaching the next field will be rewarded with a perfect example of a motte-and-bailey earthworks available for circumambulation.

2.9 Castell Gwallter at Llandre

The Gwallter (or Walter) belonging to this early form of Norman castle, where the fortifications of wood have invariably disappeared, was a dependent lord under the feudal baron Gilbert de Clare, who had bigger earthworks elsewhere in Ceredigion. Castell Gwallter is typical – we will see another on Day 3 at Sycharth (3.3). The higher hump ('motte') surrounded by the moat contained the house and barn buildings, while the flattish areas to the north and south of the moat, outside it, are the bailies, small corrals for animals. Walter de Bec had this place for only 25 years; when Henry I died in 1135, Welsh partisans from Gwynedd overwhelmed it in a flurry of resistance. It was never rebuilt, and has therefore been a 'historical site' for eight hundred years, convincing proof that the Normans did not rule the roost everywhere after 1066.

X.   Return down by the church to the railway crossing at Llandre; turn right on B4353, which soon joins A487. Soon after Bow Street (which is not a street but a village), turn left on to A4159, and left again to Penrhyn-coch on an unnumbered road. There is a sign for Dafydd ap Gwilym's birthplace in the village square, pointing east to Garth Penrhyn-coch, another at the turn-off to the left after Garth Penrhyn-coch, and a third at a final left turn near the place we are seeking.

2.10 Dafydd ap Gwilym's Birthplace, Brogynin

You will be delighted at the pleasant setting here at Brogynin, the silence, with just the sound of the stream exactly as it must have been six hundred years ago when Wales's greatest poet was born. In spite of the fact that local archaeologist D.B.Hague, visiting in 1955 the ruined cottage, then used as a pig-sty, stated that 'no part of the surviving structure can ever have sheltered the bard', we can feel Dafydd's presence in the respect that the present owner of the property (an Englishman) has shown in landscaping a small memorial space with a plaque. Besides, it was Taliesin himself who, according to a 15th century manuscript, prophesied that Brogynin would be the birthplace of a great poet.

How can we in this latter end of time begin to understand the greatness of Dafydd ap Gwilym? We can perhaps turn first to *The Story of Cardiganshire,* an old textbook for schoolchildren of the county:

> When Wales was conquered by Edward I, the Welsh bards could sing no more for many years as they had no princes and warriors whom they could flatter with songs of victory. It was Dafydd ap Gwilym who re-started the music, when he broke forth into poetry finer than that of war, by singing about birds, woods, mountains, rivers, and the beauty of nature in all its forms.

Like Chaucer, his slightly younger contemporary, Dafydd ap Gwilym wrote in the dawn of a renaissance, when new literary motifs were bursting out in Italy and France. It is proper that the plaque at Brogynin should be in French as well as English and Welsh: Dafydd undoubtedly read many French books, such as *Tales of Charlemagne.* It was not that the Norman hierarchy dominated his sensibility. There is nothing in the poetry that even hints of a downtrodden Wales. We are

Beti Rhys at Dafydd ap Gwilym's birthplace

talking of a genius ranging the literature of his time for the forms which will allow him to express his subjects, love and nature.

Primarily, love: for nature is usually a setting for love, or a refuge for the lovelorn. His range includes the Chaucerian fabliau. In his poem 'Trouble at the Inn', the narrator sees a girl in a crowded room; after everybody has retired, he tries to find her bedroom, but finds three drunken Englishmen instead: 'I beat a retreat', the poem says. 'Lucky my saints were with me. Now I ask of God forgiveness.' This is a mock self-reproach; for, to Dafydd, it is Love that is holy. Following Dante, Petrarch, and the troubadours, Dafydd ap Gwilym is the Welsh representative of the poet of love. A fellow poet, Iolo Goch, called him *hebog merched Deheubarth* ('the hawk of the girls of the South'). We imagine the fluttering as Dafydd entered Llanbadarn Church of a Sunday. In a famous passage, he tells of turning the back of his head to God in order to look at the girls some pews behind him.

All agree that Dafydd ap Gwilym was a master of the Welsh language and its poetic forms. Those of us who cannot follow here can certainly see from translations an individual in full possession of his powers, buoyant and happy, at ease with his future. There is a description of Dafydd in a Welsh manuscript dated 1587, now in the British Library – and I hope it is genuine:

> I saw in 1572 an old woman who had seen another who had conversed with Dafydd ap Gwilym. Tall and slender was he; and hair long, rippling, yellow was on him, and that full of clasps and silver rings, she said.

XI. We now make for Dafydd ap Gwilym's church, Llanbadarn Fawr. But on the way we glance at a typical manor house; for Dafydd undoubtedly had the protection and patronage of this 'uchelwyr' ('upper-class') family, or one like it.

Retrace your steps from Brogynin through Penrhyn-coch, but just before the main road (A4159) look for the right turn into the driveway of Plas Gogerddan; the sign will indicate it is now

part of the AFRC Institute of Grassland & Environmental Research. There is a circular driveway to the right.

2.11 The Manor of Plas Gogerddan

This is one of the old manor houses that had its origin with the Edwardian settlement of the 14th century. The family is descended from Rhys ap David Lloyd, who is known to have employed many bards; the Pryses have been great patrons

Plas Gogerddan

through the ages. There was always a Pryse in Parliament at Westminster, with enough of the hustler in him, so that the family maintained its wealth until the 20th century. In 1950 the University took Plas Gogerddan off their hands, and has used the land as a Welsh Plant Breeding Station.

XII.   Go straight across A4159 on the road signposted to Waun Fawr, and go over the hill and down into Llanbadarn Fawr. Look out for the square tower of the church, before reaching the main road, on the right.

2.12 The Church of Llanbadarn Fawr

The history of this religious site dedicated to St Padarn goes back very far indeed. Monastic buildings were here in the 6th century, perhaps before. E.G.Bowen in his *History of Llanbadarn*

Fawr writes of this early period:

> The monastery would be made up of a dozen or so monks under the supervision of an Abbot . . . All the monks took a vow of perfection, which included humility, obedience, almsgiving and charity. They lived in individual beehive-shaped cells and not in a single building. In addition to the monks' cells there was a little wooden, wattle and daub church, a special cell for the Abbot, a hospice or lodgings for visitors, and a kiln for drying corn before it was sent to the mill.

Bowen explains the widespread use today of the word *llan* in placenames in that this whole monastary complex was enclosed by 'an earthen wall or rampart, most often fronted by deep ditch. . . The area thus enclosed was technically the *llan* – a name which in later times was used for a church.'

All that remains now from that early *llan* are two Celtic crosses, which stood in the churchyard until 1916, when they were brought for protection into the church itself. You will notice a little seated Irishman in the panel below the main cross-head of the larger stone, which can be dated as 10th century. The smaller stone seems older, but probably is not. Legend has it that St Samson, the brother of St Padarn, was threshing with these two stones at a location about a mile from the church. The 'head' flew off and landed at Llanbadarn; annoyed, St Samson, a very strong fellow, threw the 'handle' after it.

Another story links Padarn with Maelgwn Gwynedd in a battle of wits. The king sent two servants to Llanbadarn with two sacks for safekeeping, saying they contained king's treasure. Later the servants were sent to get them back, and the sacks were found to contain only moss and gravel. Padarn demanded that the truth of the matter be settled in a trial of ordeal. Boiling water was brought and the stewards had to place their hands in it; so did Padarn. The hands of the servants were badly scalded, St Padarn's were whole and fresh. This proved he was innocent, and Maelgwn had to confess his deception; he had wanted an excuse to plunder the ecclesiastical lands. Now he was struck blind, and only received back his sight when the saint interceded upon being granted all the land between the Clarach and the Rheidol.

What we actually know of St Padarn is meagre. He was

born in Brittany of noble parents. He was on his way to Ireland to look for his father, and got as far as Llanbadarn. He had four cousins and 847 monks with him, so he founded a monastery. The present church building is dated about 1200 AD, as is the font you pass on your way in. Dafydd ap Gwilym could have been baptized in it.

2.13 The Grave of Lewis Morris (1701-1765)

A gravestone plaque in the floor of the choir of Llanbadarn church leads us to meditate for a moment on a poet – a man of letters, rather – whose works are not particularly celebrated, but whose great contribution to the Welsh life of his time is indisputable. 'He was,' says the *Oxford Companion to the Literature of Wales*, 'the prime mover in the classical revival of Welsh learning and writing during the eighteenth century.' The idea behind S4C, the Welsh language television station, had its inception with Lewis Morris, for he believed that Welsh literature would only survive if it was entertaining. So he wrote and published light verse and topical satire, and corresponded with humorous epistles among a wide network of acquaintances both home and abroad. He began his life in Anglesey as the eldest of four Morris Brothers (as they came to be called, because of their combined impact on the culture of their time). Cartographic work brought him to Aberystwyth about 1742, and lead-mining kept him in this area. He was an agent of the Crown in lead-mining licences, and also did some prospecting of his own. It was an all-round man that lies at our feet in the floor of Llanbadarn Fawr.

XIII. Looking south-west from Llanbadarn, one cannot help but be intrigued by the conspicuous peak which dominates Aberystwyth and which is topped by what could be an ancient monolith but which is really an inverted cannon from the Battle of Waterloo. No doubt this stale tribute to the Duke of Wellington will some day quietly disappear; if we now make for that summit, it is not in obeisance to a General who gloried in war but to get the feel of a much more distant and on the whole more peaceful time in history.

Backtrack a few yards to the junction where A4120 goes south, crossing the tracks of the main railway line and also those of the narrow-gauge Rheidol steam train. The road then rises steeply up to Southgate, where you turn right on A487 towards Aberystwyth. After descending for about ¼ mile, look out on the left for a sign to 'The Toll House', and turn left into the pub parking lot. Here begins the fairly gradual ascent to the top of Pen Dinas ('Summit Fortress'). Stay with the single line path (not the double cart-track) and keep the Wellington cannon in sight, and you can't go wrong.

2.14 The Hill-fort of Pen Dinas, Aberystwyth

This is a fairly accessible example of an Iron Age hill-fort, occupied by the Celts in the last three centuries BC. We passed close by several less accessible ones during the course of our day's journey: one on either side of the road out of Tal-y-bont and another practically within shouting distance above Llandre. From all three, the inhabitants could see the main centre at Pen Dinas. These were closely knit and, as far as we know, friendly communities. There is a well-known depiction of a hill-fort scene, reconstructed by the artist Alan Sorrell in *Early Wales Re-created* and reproduced elsewhere. A team of horses with paniers is being harried by the drovers up to a wooden fortified entrance and into a compound which contains several rows of round thatched houses with smoke coming from a central smoke-hole in each roof. There are sentries, but conversing women give an air of relaxation to the scene. Maybe they chose the hilltops exactly for that sense of security; perhaps also the marshy bottom-lands had something to do with it. In any case, they were not so concerned with survival that they could not also produce quite beautiful artwork in bronze. The Ceredigion Museum on Terrace Road, Aberystwyth, has some examples.

> *XIV. For the final stage of the day's outing, return to the main road (A487) and descend the rest of the way into the town across Trefechan Bridge, turning on the next left immediately after the bridge, proceeding to South Beach parking adjacent to Aberystwyth Castle.*

2.15 Aberystwyth Castle

Like all of Edward I's castles, Aberystwyth Castle is more part of English history than Welsh history. It cost the English taxpayer £4300, about the equivalent of a modern-day aircraft carrier. It was never needed in Edward's campaigns; it was blown up, using its own store of explosives, in 1649; and it is now a children's playground. Aberystwyth is in the happy situation (unlike Caernarfon, say) of being psychologically free of its castle.

Day 3

Owain Glyndŵr's Wales

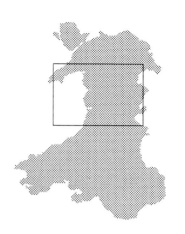

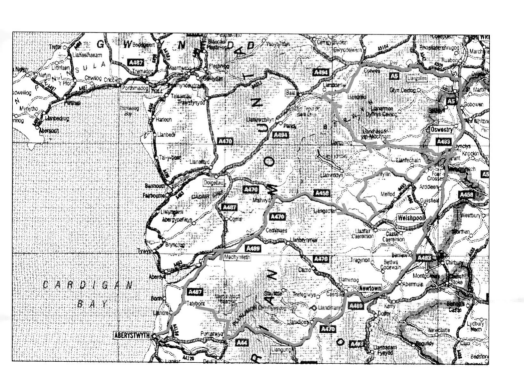

DAY 3: Owain Glyndŵr's Powys

Owain Glyndŵr has such significance in Welsh Wales that we need a whole day to explore his world.

I	From Aberystwyth on A487 to Machynlleth for Owain Glyndŵr's Parliament House (3.1)
II	Take A489 east, then A470 north (not south), then A458 east, then A495 north. Turn off on B4382 to Dolanog and Ann Griffiths's house, Dolwar Fach (3.2)
III	Proceed north through Llanfihangel-yng-Ngwynfa, and turn off B4382 onto B4393 east, joining A490 east to A495 north into Shropshire. Take B4396 west from A495, and an unnumbered road right, to Sycharth (3.3)
IV	Return to B4396 west, bearing right on to B4580 to Bishop Morgan's Llanrhaeadr-ym-Mochnant (3.4)
V	Take unnumbered road and turn right on B4391 west. After some miles and steep descent, take B4402 north, then right on B4401 to join A5 east through Corwen to Glyndŵr's Mount (3.5)
VI	From A5 take left turn on B5103, across the Dee, turning left on A542 to Valle Crucis Abbey (3.6)
VII	Take A542 east through Llangollen to join A483; keep on A483 right down to Newtown and the Robert Owen Museum (3.7)
VIII	From Newtown, take A483 (A489) west; stay on A489 until the junction with A470 south; join A44

west at Llangurig. Leave A44 at Ponterwyd on the unnumbered road to Nant-y-moch reservoir and the site of the Battle of Hyddgen (3.8) and Pumlumon Fawr (3.9)

IX *Return to Aberystwyth either by A44, or the mountain road west from Nant-y-moch to Tal-y-bont.*

I. After Llywelyn 'the Last' and 1282, Wales lost statehood. It was still a nation in spirit, but that spirit was dampened. Owain Glyndŵr was the one who fired it up again and made a valiant attempt for fifteen years to push out the English and take over the reins of government. We see him first at perhaps his most illustrious moment, presiding over his new Parliament at Machynlleth in 1404.

Take A487 north from Aberystwyth to Machynlleth. Turn right at the clocktower junction on A489, and look immediately on the left for a Tudor-style house, with the sign 'Parliament House'.

3.1 The Parliament House, Machynlleth

Military leaders usually dissolve parliaments in times of emergency. Owain Glyndŵr did the opposite; he created them – Dolgellau, Harlech, Pennal, as well as the first one at Machynlleth. Glyndŵr was a statesman, pushed forward by his birth: he would have been of the royal family of Wales if there had been an independent Wales. His parents represented lineages of both North and South Wales. He was a cultivated man of his time, as Shakespeare allows him to point out, in *Henry IV Part I*:

> For I was trained in the English court,
> Where, being but young, I framed to the harp
> Many an English ditty lovely well
> And gave the tongue an helpful ornament.

He was at the Inns of Court, making some acquaintance with Law; and had been in action in the various military campaigns available to an enterprising young aristocrat, in Scotland, Flanders, perhaps Ireland and France. His reputation is given in Shakespeare as that of

> a worthy gentleman
> Exceeding well read, and profited
> In strange concealments, valiant as a lion,
> And wondrous affable, and as bountiful
> As mines of India.

The 'Parliament House' should be taken as a symbolic site: the present building is judged by experts to be more recent than the 15th century; and in any case Owain would have required more space than the room you enter for all the dignitaries from France, Scotland and Spain and their retinues to gather to give witness to his formal declaration of sovereignty. It must have been in marquees and the open air that 'the proud little town of Machynlleth' (as the pamphlet puts it) hosted 'the glittering colourful ceremony with his standard of the golden dragon which had fluttered so thrillingly on Hyddgen mountain, now bravely holding pride of place . . . Never, neither before nor since, has the quiet little place witnessed such a scene of

Entrance to the Parliament House

enthusiasm, fervour, and colour.' So it might have been reported in the *Cambrian News* of the time. But there was also serious business to be done; and, for instance, Owain here concluded an alliance with the French, sealing the parchment with the four lions of Llywelyn the Great (the document and seal still exist in Paris). Of course, this Parliament was something of a showcase, a parading of feudal prides and compliances, rather than a democratic decision-making body. But it could never have happened unless (as is always the case generally in guerrilla warfare) the people of the countryside had not supported the uprising fully. By the end of the year Glyndŵr ruled Wales right to Offa's Dyke.

David Davies MP, the philanthropist, restored the structure in 1912, and handed it over to the Machynlleth Urban District Council. Notice the mural of Glyndŵr's battle of Hyddgen by artist Murray Urquart on the wall of the Reading Room of the Institute. We will reach that spot on the mountain slopes of Pumlumon by the end of this day's tour.

> *II. Proceed on A489 (east) from Machynlleth; keep left at the Cemaes junction, taking A470 north (not south); branch off at Mallwyd east on A458. A coffee REST STOP on A458 is Dyffryn Restaurant; look out for the sign 'Restaurant' on the left, and pull into the car park.*
>
> *This Glyndŵr day will be interspersed with two or three quieter figures, and we are now about to make a small detour to the house where a poetess lived and the churchyard where she was buried.*
>
> *Take the A495 towards Oswestry from A458, and after about 2 miles look for the B4382 signpost to Dolanog for a left turn. In Dolanog, if you follow the sign 'Free car park & toilet', it brings you to the first of the memorials to Ann Griffiths, a chapel, with a plaque to her dated 1903. Proceed along B4382 until on the left appear the two distinctive white gate posts of 'Dolwar Fach'; enter and drive up into the farm yard. Ann Griffiths's house is the well-kept stone farm house through the black-painted gate. Visitors are welcome.*

3.2 Dolwar Fach, Ann Griffiths's House

The plaque on the memorial chapel at Dolanog calls Ann Griffiths 'Prif Emynyddes Cymru' ('The Foremost Female Hymnwriter of Wales'). In spite of the fact that only about thirty of her hymns have been preserved, Ann Griffiths achieved such feeling and intensity in her verses that she is put on a par with those who wrote several hundred. Saunders Lewis is quoted as saying that one of her hymns was 'one of the greatest religious poems in any European language.' She is admired for 'her sharp intellect and her deep sensitivity' and 'the gift of clothing abstract ideas in rhythmic melodious language.' Outside of the revivalist atmosphere in which words like 'grace' and 'choice' were discussed with great passion, we may find it difficult to feel the power of the 'clothed' abstractions. But listen to the imagery of one of her best known verses:

56

Gwna fi fel pren planedig, O! fy Nuw,
(Make me as a tree planted, Oh! my God,)

Yn ir ar lan afonydd dyfroedd byw:
(Sappy on the bank of the rivers of the waters of life:)

Yn gwreiddio ar led, a'i ddail heb wywo mwy,
(Rooting widely, its leaves without withering any more,)

Yn ffrwytho dan gawodydd dwyfol glwy.
(Fructifying under the showers of a divine wound.)

Jane Aaron has called our attention to what she calls 'the blissful physicality' of these images, which probably contain more sexuality than the poet herself was consciously aware of. Again:

Cofia, Arglwydd, dy ddyweddi,
(Remember, Lord, thy betrothed,)

Llama ati fel yr hydd.
(Leap towards her like a stag.)

Ann Griffiths was born here in 1776. She had little schooling, and knew only Welsh. She was a lively farmer's daughter; and it was actually when she was on her way to a dance that she was persuaded by an old family servant to stop and listen to a visiting Independent preacher, Benjamin Jones of Pwllheli. Ann was deeply moved, and consulted her parish priest. His ugly attitude to the Methodists only succeeded in driving her over to their camp. She travelled often the thirty or forty miles to Bala to receive communion from Thomas Charles, and repeated word for word his sermons to her friends upon her return. It was to this house, Dolwar Fach, that she always returned, to work and to ponder in her room. She did not write down her hymns. It is one of the marvellous circumstances surrounding this short-lived poetess that she only recited them to the house-maid, Ruth Evans, who turned out to have the kind of memory that could retain them for several years until, after Ann's death, she passed them on to Thomas Charles, who had them printed.

It was to this house that Ann came with her husband, whom she married a year after her father's death. A year later she gave birth to a child that died; she herself never recovered from that birth, and died in 1805 at the age of 29. The Jones family now in residence at the house took it over at that time.

You will sign a Visitors Book started after the visit of O.M.Edwards, which he memorialized in his *Cartrefi Cymru* ('Homesteads of Wales'). You will have an opportunity to purchase by donation a pamphlet *Ann Griffiths: A short History of Ann and her Chapels,* the proceeds from which go to restore the chapel at nearby Pontrobert, which was Ann's spiritual home. Since the Methodist movement had not yet received the right to bury its members, Ann's grave is at the Parish Church of St Michael, Llanfihangel-yng-Ngwynfa, just on the left inside the churchyard gates. The setting of this church in an exquisite wind-blown landscape gives some idea why religion and beauty are brought together in Ann Griffiths's poetry. It is well worth seeing.

> *Proceed north on B4382 from Dolwar Fach gates; turn right at the 'Parking' sign in the village of Llanfihangel-yng-Ngwynfa, and drive up the few yards to the church gates.*

> *III. After this detour into another time and mood, we resume our search for Owain Glyndŵr by making for Sycharth, his probable birthplace, but a shrine without signpost or plaque.*
>
> *Proceed north from Llanfihangel-yng-Ngwynfa, and turn right on B4393 (through Llanfyllin), joining A490 east to A495 north (towards Oswestry). After 1½ miles into Shropshire look out for B4396 off to the left (signposted to Bala). After going west for about 2 miles, look for a signpost on the left-hand side of the road in the hedge, which indicates the side road off to the right to Llansilin. (This is just before the border. If you pass it and get to the border, turn back and take the first left.) On this unnumbered road, bear left at the first junction, pass two roads leading off to the right, and stop at the third, which is a farm track leading up to a house and a gate. (Be prepared to stop as soon as you see the white farmhouse facing you in the middle distance above the road. If you pass the place, you will come to a humpback bridge over a stream, where you will see*

a sign 'The Old Blacksmith, Sycharth'. Turn around and return.) You may not see it immediately, but there is a sign indicating that the farm track up to the gate is a public footpath. Enter the gate, and the motte-and bailey shape of the Sycharth homestead is readily discerned.

3.3 Glyndŵr's Birthplace, Sycharth

As one walks round the perimeter of the moat, one realises that this is one of the most impressively beautiful locations in Wales for a home. It was one of two houses owned by Glyndŵr's family, and tradition has it that he was born and raised here. We have a vivid contemporary description of the atmosphere of a bustling manor house presided over by a munificent host in a poem 'Sycharth' by the bard Iolo Goch, given here in Joseph Clancy's translation:

> To his court in haste I'll go,
> The two hundred best worthies,
> A baron's court, high manners,
> With many bards, a fine life,
> Lord of great Powys, Maig's land,
> The one whom true hope longs for.
> Look at its form and fashion,
> Moated with water's gold round,
> Fine manor, bridge on the moat,
> A hundred-pack-wide portal,
> In couples, a coupled work,
> Each of the couples coupled,
> Patrick's belfry, fruit of France,
> Westminster's smooth-linked cloister.
> Clasped the same is each corner,
> Gold sanctum, a perfect whole.
>
> Bands in the hillside above
> Side by side like a dungeon
> And each, like a knot tied tight,
> Interlocked with the other.
> Nine-fold mould, eighteen chambers,
> Green hilltop, fine-timbered house.
> On four marvellous pillars
> Close to heaven is his hall.
> On each firm wooden pillar
> A loft on the sturdy croft,
> And four lofts, delightful,
> Are linked, there the minstrels sleep,

Four splendid lofts, converted,
A fine well-filled nest, to eight.
Tile roofs on the tall houses,
Chimneys that cannot nurse smoke,
Nine halls in matching pattern,
And nine wardrobes in each one,
Fine shops with comely contents,
Well-stocked shop like London's Cheap.

Cross-tipped church, clean lime-white walls,
Chapels and fair glass windows.

The site of Sycharth

Each side full, each house at court,
Orchard, vineyard, white fortress;
The master's rabbit warren;
Ploughs and strong steeds of great fame;
Near the court, even finer,
The deer park within that field;
Fresh green meadows and hayfields;
Neatly enclosed rows of grain;
Fine mill on smooth-flowing stream;
Dove-cot, a bright stone tower;
A fish-pond, enclosed and deep,
Where nets are cast when need be,
Abounding, no argument,
In pike and splendid whiting;
His land a board where birds dwell,
Peacocks, high-stepping herons.

His serfs do their proper work,
Fill the needs of the region,
Bringing Shrewsbury's new beer,
Spirits, the first-brewed bragget,

All drinks, white bread and wine,
His meat, fire for his kitchen.
Tent of bards from all regions,
All welcomed there, every day.
The best wife among women,
I'm blest by her wine and mead,
A knightly line's bright daughter,
Proud hostess of royal blood.
His children come, two by two,
A fine nestful of princes.

Seldom has there been seen there
Either a latch or a lock,
Or someone playing porter,
No lack of bountiful gifts,
No need, no hunger, no shame,
No one is parched at Sycharth.
The best Welshman, bold leader,
Owns this land, Pywer Lew's line,
Slim strong man, the land's finest,
And owns this court, place to praise.

One can see why G.M.Trevelyan, the noted historian, could
describe Glyndŵr as 'this wonderful man, an attractive and
unique figure in a period of debased and selfish politics.'
Sycharth, as Iolo Goch gives it to us in his poem, is the epitome
of the free and full life which Owain had to leave in order to
defend its integrity. The place was burnt to the ground by the
English in 1403.

**IV. Proceed on over the humpback bridge, turn right (towards
Llansilin), then turn left on to B4580 leading to Llanrhaeadr-
ym-Mochnant. Park by the church wall.**

3.4 William Morgan's Parish Church, Llanrhaeadr-ym-Mochnant

At the gateway to the church, Eglwys Sant Dogfan, are two
plaques, one giving William Morgan's dates, 1545-1604, with a
quotation, the first words of the Bible as he translated them;
the other indicating that it was while he was the vicar of this
parish that Morgan finished the translation in 1588 after ten
years' work. Inside the church you will find a William Morgan

Bible on the lectern: you are bound to, since his is the translation used to this day. We will visit the William Morgan birthplace later (4.9), but this is the remote village in which he did his great work.

> This is where he sought God.
> And found him? The centuries
> Have been content to follow
> Down passages of serene prose.
> (R.S.Thomas, 'Llanrhaeadr-ym-Mochnant')

The church of William Morgan

The famous falls are four miles up a side road, but the village of Llanrhaeadr-ym-Mochnant ('Place of the waterfall of the pig valley') is a lovely compact place to stroll around. Go as far as the bridge over Afon Rhaeadr. REST STOP meals at the Wynnstay Arms, or the Cegin Fach with a varied menu.

V. Out of Llanrhaeadr-ym-Mochnant, take the unnumbered road signposted to Bala. At Pen-y-bont-fawr, turn right on B4391 west towards Bala. After a long fast drive, there is a steep winding descent before the turn-off right on B4402 (towards Corwen). Soon, past Pale, there is another right turn, on to B4401, the road through Llandrillo. Just before Corwen, the road joins A5. Turn right and proceed east through the town.

One knows one has entered Glyndŵr country when one sees the Owain Glyndŵr Hotel (renamed from 'The New Inn'). It was probably in Corwen that Glyndŵr first massed his army in 1401, remembering that his namesake Owain Gwynedd outfaced Henry II here in 1166. We are looking for the site of Owain's other ancestral home.

Proceed along A5 about 2 miles from Corwen, viewing the picturesque village of Carrog on the other side of the River Dee. Just past the bridge to Carrog a hillock appears above the left-hand side of the road, distinguished only by a bunch of scraggly trees. Unless you go slowly (which is not usual for A5) you may miss this site, and there is no pull-out for parking.

3.5 Owain Glyndŵr's Mount, near Glyndyfrdwy

We cannot be too concerned at not having access to this treed mound, because the Glyndŵr house's exact location is uncertain, perhaps 250 yards to the east of the mound, further down towards the fast-flowing Dee (Dyfrdwy). In any case, there was a house, and in it Owain was first proclaimed 'Prince of Wales' among a gathering of relatives and supporters. This first act of rebellion against the English crown was on 16 September 1400, a day of the year that will no doubt become recognized as a national holiday in Wales.

The grievance that triggered the rebellion was over a piece of land. Owain's neighbour Reginald Grey, Lord of Ruthin, was in with the new king Henry IV, whereas Owain had been close to the deposed Richard II. The historian Pennant has described the particulars of the dispute:

> When Henry went on his expedition against the Scots, Owain was to have been summoned, among the barons, to attend the king with his vassals. The writ for that purpose was entrusted to Reginald Grey, who designedly neglected to deliver it till the time was nearly elapsed, and it became impossible for Owain to obey. Reginald returned to the king and misrepresented the absence of Owain as an act of wilful disobedience; and by this piece of treachery, took possession of all his land; and under pretence of forfeiture, invaded such parts of Glyndŵr's estates as lay adjacent to his own.

63

Owain's pride prevented him from crawling to the king, so he chose the opposite: to live up to the role of disloyal rebel that had been thrust upon him so meanly. He could now be true to his Welsh royal blood, and owe allegiance to no one. Of course, this one incident would not have caused the flare-up it did if it was not that other such rebuffs of the Welsh population at large had not been smouldering. Gwynfor Evans tells what happened after Glyndŵr's call to arms:

> The little army marched through Rhuthun, the town of Lord Grey, and burnt it down. A thousand years after the arrival of Cunedda in Wales and fourteen centuries after Caradog's brave defence, Glyndŵr went to war to restore to Wales its liberty. He attacked the English boroughs of Denbigh, Rhuddlan, Flint, Hawarden and Holt; then on to Oswestry and Welshpool. After this the armies of the nearby English counties met and defeated them, but not until Henry had commanded the armies of the ten counties to assemble at Shrewsbury.

We will not follow Glyndŵr's war in detail. We have already looked at one important battle, Pilleth (1.2), and will visit Hyddgen at the end of this day's tour (3.8). The importance of the rebellion is that it existed at all, and that it remains in the minds of present-day nationalists. It is also significant that no monument or plaque exists either here or at Sycharth: the Establishment still seems rather apprehensive about Owain.

Glyndyfrdwy, once the name of the wide estate owned by the Glyndŵr family as feudal lords has now been given to a small village on A5 and its railway stop (now defunct). 'Glyndŵr Hall' in the village is merely a social meeting place, of no historical or political significance.

VI. Proceed east on A5 through Glyndyfrdwy; look out for a left turn B5103 signposted to Ruthin (Rhuthun). Once across the river, keep right, up to the junction with A542, where you take the left turn towards Ruthin (north). You will soon see a sign for Valle Crucis Abbey and the ruins themselves on the right-hand side of the road. There is parking space near the entrance booth (small entry fee).

3.6 Valle Crucis Abbey, Burialplace of Owain's Bard

These are impressive remains of an abbey founded in 1201 by Madog ap Gruffudd Maelor, ruler of northern Powys in his time. It retains its Latin name ('Abbey of the Valley of the Cross') and an atmosphere of intrusion: the imperialism of the Cistercian order, with its centre in France, was such that, in order to meet the rule that their abbeys be in unpopulated areas, they had the inhabitants of this valley removed to another part of Madog's lordship – a sort of early case of 'flooding out' a Welsh community.

It has long been understood in oral tradition that one of the six graves in the choir of the chapel is that of Iolo Goch, Owain Glyndŵr's bard. Recent scholarship puts his death at 1398, so that he was not the war poet that he was once taken to be. His vision of Owain's fame did not depend upon military deeds but, as we have seen with the poem 'Sycharth', was praise for his good governance and the blessings of ordinary life.

There is another connection, in a story which comes from the mists of time. The Abbot of Valle Crucis was once walking at dawn in the hills above the Abbey. He met Owain Glyndŵr there, who said: 'You have risen early, father.' 'No,' was the Abbot's reply. 'It is you who have risen early, by a hundred years.'

VII.   Go back along A542 east, and proceed to Llangollen. The only response to the traffic jams of Llangollen is to stop there. Cross the bridge, and follow signs to the city car park. The lounge of the Royal Hotel, overlooking the river, makes a good REST STOP.

We will now cross over into England for a quick road north to south. There is no such road within the borders of Wales; this has been the subject of petitions and protests to Westminster, but it strikes me as a happy state of affairs. (I believe communications in West Wales should be by coastal packet ships and hovercraft of the quieter variety.) On this English route we pass quickly by Chirk and Powys Castles, which

Owain also had to take a pass on.

Leave Llangollen east on A5, which merges into A483 south. Stay on A483 through Oswestry, all the way down to Newtown (Y Drenewydd). Go into the centre of the business district, and find the Robert Owen Memorial Museum at a prominent corner.

3.7 Robert Owen Memorial Museum, Newtown

Robert Owen, the great social reformer, was born in Newtown in 1771, but was apprenticed in Lincolnshire at the age of ten. His precocious business sense advanced him quickly, and at twenty-seven he found himself the manager of a big cotton mill in New Lanark, Scotland, and married to the boss's daughter. His efforts to rid industry of the abuse of child labour and to introduce profit-sharing by the workers are well known. Owen cannot be thought of as a Welsh 'nation-builder', except indirectly. T.E.Ellis MP praised him in these words:

> It is significant that the initiator in Britain of the movement for collective and municiple activity in the common effort for the common good was Robert Owen, who embraced in these latter days the spirit of the old Welsh social economy. He was born at Newtown, whither, after a strenuous career, he came to die. There is something striking in the fact that among those who escorted the remains of Robert Owen to their long home were the schoolchildren of Drenewydd . . .

This is from Tom Ellis's famous lecture at Bangor in 1892, 'The Memory of the Kymric Dead'. With this pleasant museum in the centre of his birth town, Owen has the memorial that Ellis was demanding.

VIII. Take A483 (A489) out of Newtown, and stay on A489 until its junction with A470; turn left and go south on A470 through Llanidloes to join A44 west at Llangurig. This is the road of our first day entry into Wales. This time, coming down from the mountains to the village of Ponterwyd, look for a road to the right signposted to the Nant-y-moch reservoir. Drive along this unnumbered road about 3 miles, and park at the damsite.

> *The plaque unveiled here at Nant-y-moch dam on 16 July 1976 by Gwynfor Evans commemorates Owain Glyndŵr's victory at the Battle of Hyddgen. To see the battlefield proper, you will have to go further, as far as Maesnant, the small house built for two brothers who were rendered homeless by the waters of the dam.*
>
> *Drive on the dirt road on the east side of the reservoir until it ends. Then it is a short walk to the next stream, from where you can see the white stones (Cerrig Cyfamod Glyndŵr, 'Stones of the Covenant of Glyndŵr') which the eye can follow north to the confluence of Afon Hyddgen, the scene of the battle.*

3.8 The Battlefield of Hyddgen, Pumlumon

Local tradition has Owain spending the night before the battle with his men gathered at a sheltered spot in the foothills of the eastern side of the valley, called 'Siambr Trawsfynydd' ('Chamber Across-Mountain'). Deulwyn Morgan had the Ordnance Survey put this name on their maps some years ago, but when we recently tried to find the place it became clear that the Forestry Commission, in building a new road, had filled in the *siambr*. On the authority of Cledwyn Vaughan and our own guess as to Owain's strategy, we can say that the fighting itself took place in the middle of the valley on a flat called Esgair Ffordd ('Ridge Way'), though Cledwyn Vaughan also says that local tradition has the footprints of Owain's horse, Llwyd-y-Bacsie, higher up at the top of Craig-y-march.

The sole written source is the Peniarth manuscript 135 in the National Library, the *Annals of Owain Glyndŵr* by the poet Gruffydd Hiraethog. J.E.Lloyd translated the pertinent passage as follows:

> Owain rose with 120 reckless men and robbers and he brought them in warlike fashion to the uplands of Ceredigion; and 1500 men of the lowlands of Ceredigion and of Rhos and Penfro assembled there and came to the mountain with the intent to seize Owain. The encounter between them was on Hyddgen Mountain, and no sooner did the English troops turn their backs in flight than

200 of them were slain. Owain now won great fame, and a great number of youths and fighting men from every part of Wales rose and joined him, until he had a great host at his back.

Yes, there were battles; but the bloodthirsty Owain Glyndŵr is not the whole story. I asked Beti Rhys of Aberystwyth (formerly of the bookstore in Cardiff) what Owain meant to her. She replied: 'He wanted two universities in Wales, and the Welsh church independent from England.' This is Owain the Reformer. The fact is that small independencies have been achieved in Wales, and it is clear that they would not have been achieved without the kind of stubbornness Owain exhibited.

Gwynfor Evans at the unveiling of the plaque at Nant-y-moch undoubtedly expressed sentiments similar to those in *Land of My Fathers* (pp.270-271), where he sums up Glyndŵr and what he means to the Welsh nationalist of today:

> The followers of Glyndŵr remained faithful to the end. In 1415 Gruffudd Young was still working for him in France; it was he who maintained in the Council of Constance, the assembly which ended the scandal of papal schism, that the Welsh were a nation and that they should have a vote there. There was not one attempt to supplant Owain as leader throughout his career, nor one attempt to betray him at the end of his life. Not one Welsh word of criticism of him has survived from that century. It is known that he was not alive in 1417, but no one knows where he died. He disappeared in dignified silence. The poets refused to believe that he was dead; so not one of them composed an elegy to his memory. To them, and to a host of Welsh people, he will never die. His spirit lives on like an unquenchable flame, a symbol of the determination of the Welsh to live as a free nation.
>
> The Welsh believed he would return when needed by his people. His spirit is needed today. As the nation matures in loyalty towards its own country, it can echo the words used by Dafydd Iwan in his great song:
>
> Myn Duw, mi wn y daw. By God, I know he will come.

3.9 Cai and Bedwyr's Seat, Pumlumon Fawr

As you stand facing Hyddgen, the slope to your right leads up to the highest summit of Pumlumon Fawr.

> As Kai and Bedwyr sat on a beacon carn on the summit of Plinlimmon, in the highest wind that ever was in the world, they looked around them, and saw a great smoke towards the south,

afar off, which did not bend in the wind . . .

And so, via Lady Charlotte Guest's nice old translation of *The Mabinogion,* we are off into medieval romance, itself an echo of older stories that have attached themselves to these hills. (Cledwyn Vaughan knows where the giant's campfire was, whose smoke Cai and Bedwyr saw.)

IX. To reach Aberystwyth, you can retrace your steps to A44. Alternatively, there is the more interesting if more trying route, following the dirt road around the west side of the reservoir, over Bryn Gwyn, and ultimately into Tal-y-bont, whence A487 into Aberystwyth.

Day 4

Domains of the
North Wales Princes

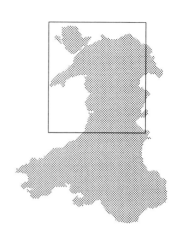

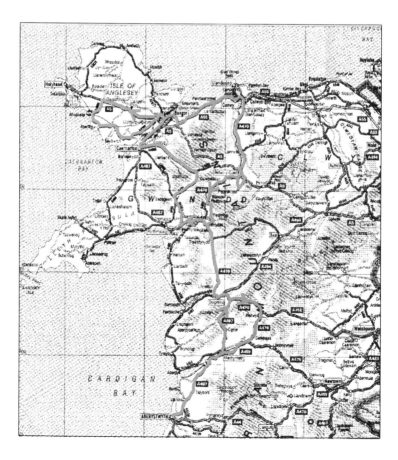

DAY 4: Domains of the Northern Princes

We will seek out the majesty and serenity of the courts of the kingdom of Gwynedd.

I	From Aberystwyth on A487 to Machynlleth and on to Cross Foxes, north on A470, bypassing Dolgellau, to Trawsfynydd, picking up A487 again through Maentwrog, turning off on B4410 to Garreg and A4085 north to Beddgelert, thence on A498 to the junction with A4086, turning up the Llanberis Pass, and down to Llyn Padarn and Dolbadarn Castle (4.1)
II	Proceed north on A4086. Near Caernarfon, take a by-pass to A4085 north to the Roman Fort of Segontium (4.2)
III	Go through Caernarfon town centre on A4085, and leave on A487 up to A5 west over Menai Straits into Anglesey; take A4080 south to the coast and Aberffraw (4.3)
IV	Resume A4080 to the church at Llangadwaladr (4.4)
V	Proceeding on A4080, turn right to visit the burial chamber of Bryn-celli-ddu (4.5) and left to visit Plas Newydd (4.6)
VI	Join A5 east, by-passing Bangor, to the junction with A55 east; exit at Abergwyngregyn (4.7)
VII	Resume A55 east, by-passing Conwy; exit on A470 south to Llanrwst and the Gwydir Chapel

(4.8)

VIII *(Optional segment) From Llanrwst on A470 to A5 east to the B4406 turn-off to Penmachno; follow sign to Tŷ Mawr, birthplace of William Morgan (4.9) – proceeding onward to cross the River Lledr and join A470 west*

IX *A470 (from Llanrwst to Blaenau Ffestiniog) passes Dolwyddelan Castle (4.10)*

X *Proceed south on A470, with optional stop at the Llechwedd Slate Caverns (4.11)*

XI *Take A470 south through Blaenau Ffestiniog, Ffestiniog, Dolgellau, and Dinas Mawddwy to Cemaes junction, where A489 goes to Machynlleth, whence A487 to Aberystwyth*

I. We need an early start, before the traffic, to get us quickly up to Snowdonia and the haunts of the Gwynedd princes. The road at first is familiar.

Take A487 through Machynlleth and north to Cross Foxes, where A470 takes over, by-passes Dolgellau, and proceeds north to Trawsfynydd. Just past the power station you will see the number A487 again, branching off to the west. Take A487 through Maentwrog, across Afon Dwyryd, and look out on the right for B4410 (signposted Tan-y-bwlch and Rhyd), the short-cut route to Garreg, where it connects with A4085. Turn right and take A4085 north to Beddgelert, turning there on A498 (towards Capel Curig). We are now entering Snowdonia proper (Eryri), and various scenic viewpoints will invite you to stop. At the junction with A4086, turn left and drive up the astounding Llanberis Pass. Reaching the lake Llyn Padarn, look out for the sign to Dolbadarn Castle on the right, and turn into the car park.

4.1 Dolbadarn Castle, Snowdonia

I am perfectly convinced that Dolbadarn Castle and most other Welsh-built castles were constructed as residences and with an eye to the view. Unlike Edward's castles, they were not there to dominate the terrain but to enjoy it. They were fortified enough to be a safe retreat if anybody wanted to chase you that far; but I bet they were also homey. Not that one would want to be imprisoned in one for twenty years, as Owain Goch was, having got on the wrong side of his brother Llywelyn ap Gruffydd. J.M.W.Turner painted Dolbadarn Castle with Owain in mind, writing the following lines for an exhibition catalogue:

> How aweful is the silence of the waste,
> Where nature lifts her mountains to the sky.
> Majestic solitude, behold the tower
> Where hopeless Owain, long imprison'd, pin'd,
> And wrung his hands for liberty, in vain.

This is nineteenth century Romanticism. Owain knew why he

was there, and probably thought himself rather lucky to have house arrest in such a beautiful spot. Given the politics of the time, he had literally nowhere outside to go. There is a nice balance in the fact that, though Edward took woodwork from Dolbadarn for his monster of a castle at Caernarfon, enough of the place was left for Owain Glyndŵr to use it as an Alcatraz for his enemy Reginald Grey of Ruthin, while waiting for the ransom money.

II.   We will be ignoring, deliberately, Edward's Caernarfon Castle, but we do not want to ignore the Roman Segontium on the outskirts of the city. As we have mentioned before, the effect of the Roman era in Wales was to enhance Celtic culture not to destroy it. Segontium is modest in comparison with the Castle down below.

Proceed from Llanberis down A4086. We need to get over to A4085 to the west, and we can do so on a by-pass route (unnumbered), a left turn as one reaches the suburbs of Caernarfon. Once on Beddgelert Road (A4085) going towards the city centre, look out for a rather small sign on a lamp-post on the right-hand side of the road. The Welsh is first:

Caer Rufeinig
Segontium
Roman Fort.

(If you miss the sign, you will still notice the excavated outlines of the old Roman buildings on the immediate right of the road.) Park on the roadside and enter the museum with a small fee.

4.2 The Roman Remains of Segontium, Caernarfon

As Gwynfor Evans has pointed out in his pamphlet *Magnus Maximus and the Birth of the Welsh Nation*, the last of the Roman generals at Segontium left such a powerful memory that he got into medieval Welsh legend in 'The Dream of Magnus Maximus'. The dream was of Snowdonia and a princess (Elen of the Sarn Helen roads). The true story is perhaps more interesting than the romance. Maximus was from Spain, from Galicia where a Celtic language was spoken. He seems to have felt at home in our corner of the Empire; he may have married here. When he left Wales and crossed to France, in 383 AD, he did so under the banner of the Red Dragon. Mortimer Wheeler, the excavator of Segontium, found that intensive occupation ceased at that time. Roman influence in Wales was almost over. But Maximus had done well by the native Celts, using many of them in responsible positions in the defence systems against the Picts and the Irish, which defences remained intact and well-manned for years after. As Gwynfor Evans has said in *Land of My Fathers* of Magnus Maximus or Macsen Wledig (as his name is written in Welsh):

> Probably Macsen's greatest achievement for the Welsh, and the one which made the deepest impression on them, was the formal transference to them of the responsibilty for defending their own country. Thus the people of the states of Wales were now recognised as responsible people within the Empire, in effect dependent solely upon themselves, with no Roman soldier on their soil. The legions at Chester and Caerleon had moved nearer to eastern England to strengthen the defence against the attacks being made there. Perhaps the other forts in Wales had seen no Roman soldiers for a long time, though England was to remain under Roman rule for a generation after Macsen left. After three centuries of Roman oversight the Welsh were once again – as they had been for centuries before the Caesars – completely responsible for their own existence, the first people within the Empire to become self-governing.

III. Proceed down A4085, through Caernarfon city centre, and leave by A487 towards Bangor, and follow the signs for Holyhead (A5) over the Menai (new) bridge into Ynys Môn (Anglesey). After about 10 miles on A5, look for a turn-off left on A4080 towards the coast and Aberffraw. Stop at the renovated farm now called Llys Llywelyn, where you will find a locally-run café for a REST STOP.

4.3 Aberffraw of the Princes, Ynys Môn

It was here, according to the *Mabinogi,* that Branwen, daughter of Llŷr of Britain, married the son of the King of Ireland:

> And they fixed upon Aberffraw as the place where she should become his bride. And they went thence, and towards Aberffraw the hosts proceeded; Matholwch and his host in their ships, Bendigeid Vran and his host by land, until they came to Aberffraw. And at Aberffraw they began the feast and sat down. And thus sat they. The King of the Island of the Mighty and Manawyddan the son of Llŷr, on one side, and Matholwch on the other side, and Branwen the daughter of Llŷr beside him. And they were not within a house, but under tents. No house could ever contain Bendigeid Vran. And they began the banquet and caroused and discoursed. And when it was more pleasing to them to sleep than to carouse, they went to rest, and that night Branwen became Matholwch's bride.
>
> And next day they arose, and all they of the Court, and the officers began to equip and to range the horses and the attendants, and they ranged them in order as far as the sea.

The fact that the *Mabinogi* 'Branwen' story places a royal court at Aberffraw supports historical records that indicate it was the chief court of the princes of Gwynedd. Llywelyn the Great used the title *'Tywysog Aberffraw ac Arglwydd Eryri'* ('Prince of Aberffraw and Lord of Snowdonia'). Llywelyn 'the Last' was described in a famous elegy as *'frenin, dderwin ddor, Aberffraw'* ('king, an oaken door, of Aberffraw'). It is also thought that Cunedda, the first prince, founded Aberffraw; but of all this activity, from first to last of the princes, you will see no trace in the present hamlet. In places like this it is what you cannot see that makes it worth the journey; it is what you can feel, a charm in the air largely undisturbed by the centuries.

If you want to see where the archaeologists think that the *llys* 'court' must have been, you will take a short walk (or drive) out of the centre of the village.

> *Follow the road signposted to Eglwys Cwyfan. In less than ½ mile, the road bends left at a white 'Gatehouse' on the right-hand side of the road. At this spot, looking down to the water over the hedge, you will see the field where the old fortifications are thought to have been and where the horse and attendants of Bendigeidfran ranged in the marriage*

procession down to the sea.

*IV. Resume A4080 east towards Newborough, after about 2
miles reaching the village of Llangadwaladr. Find the small
church of St Cadwaladr, just off the highway.*

4.4 The Carved Stone of Llangadwaladr

The church may be locked, so you may have to leave without
seeing the carved stone which is further evidence for the
ancient importance of this area. The inscription is
CATAMANUS REX SAPIENTISIMUS OPINATEIMUS
OMNIUM REGUM, that is 'Cadman the King, wisest and most
renowed of all kings' – referring to King Cadfan who died
about 625 AD, the grandfather of the Cadwaladr after whom
the village is named. It is, says Gwynfor Evans, 'the most
magnificent inscription that is found on any ancient stone in
Wales.'

> There are other memorial stones still standing in Gwynedd. The
> inscription is always in Latin – one refers to a 'a citizen of
> Gwynedd', another to a justice of the peace, others to priests, and
> one to a physician, 'Nelius Medicus', which shows that the medical
> profession was held in high regard in Gwynedd. The Penmachno
> inscription tantalisingly records that the memorial was made 'in
> the time of Justinus the Consul'. Justinus was Consul in 540.
> Altogether these stones reflect a civilised and sophisticated society.

And also, of course, a militaristic society, since in the
middle ages in Wales, as anywhere else, political leaders had
to be military men. In Gwynfor's words: 'war was the only
way men knew to change and defend the political order.'

*V. A4080 east joins A5 at that place of the very long name,
Llanfairpwllgwyngyllgogerychwyrndrobwll-llantysilio-
gogogoch, which approximately translates as 'St Mary's
Church in the hollow of the white hazel near a rapid whirlpool
and the church of St Tysilio near the red cave'. Just prior to
Llanfair P.G. (as it is sometimes abbreviated), there are two*

worthy tourist attractions, Bryn-celli-ddu, a very striking and accessible ancient burial chamber, and Plas Newydd, a manor house preserved by the National Trust.

Following A4080 around the south end of Anglesey, keeping Menai Straits on one's right, look out on the left for the road to the burial chamber: there is a signpost to Llanddaniel, with a large brown sign to a 'Golf Complex', and below that, a small green sign to Bryn-celli-ddu ('Mound of the Grove Sombre').

4.5 Bryn-celli-ddu Burial Chamber

This is one of the best examples in Europe of a burial chamber of around 2000 BC. Excavated in 1928, it is now in state care. There should not be any trouble entering and exploring the site; but if it should be locked, ask at the nearby farmhouse.

4.6 The National Trust's Plas Newydd

Well marked and clearly seen on the right of the road (A4080) soon after the Bryn-celli-ddu turn-off is the ornate contrast, Plas Newydd, a late 19th century *nouveau riche* house with a famous mural and many trappings not to be found at Bryn-celli-ddu. It belonged to the marquesses of Anglesey until 1976, when it was taken over by the National Trust.

VI.   Join A5 east (towards Betws-y-coed), by-passing Bangor. Leave A5, following signs to Conwy (A55). This road along the shore of Conwy Bay is a fast four-lane highway; exit at Abergwyngregyn ('Aber' on some maps), where one can see Tyn-y-Mwd at the centre of the village, tree-topped, behind houses opposite the church.

4.7 Siwan of Abergwyngregyn

What remains of one of the great fortified houses of the princes is now only a mound of the motte-and-bailey type. In its day it was a centre of power, built by Llywelyn the Great; it was here in 1282 that Llywelyn 'the Last' received and spurned Edward I's demands, which refusal quickly led to the final onslaught on Wales.

The place is remembered in another context. Llywelyn the Great's wife Joan (Siwan, in Welsh) is said to have become infatuated with a noble prisoner here, William de Breos, a Marcher lord; and, according to the story, it was a situation like Tristan and Isolde. Siwan, the daughter of King John of England, was as though victim of a love potion. De Breos was ransomed and had to leave, and Siwan was shameless in her sorrow. Llywelyn 'cordially' invited him back for a visit. This emotional tale has him hanging de Breos and showing his lifeless corpse to Siwan. When Llywelyn sent his bard to summon Siwan, the following exchange is what traditionally took place:

> Diccyn, diccyn gwraig Llywelyn,
> Beth a roit am weled Gwilym?
> ('Tell me, tell me, wife of Llywelyn,
> What would you give for a sight of your William?')
>
> Cymru, Lloegr a Llywelyn,
> Oll a rown am weled Gwilym!
> ('Wales, England, and Llywelyn,
> All would I give to see my William!')

Siwan is then brought to the gibbet, and sees what was swinging from it. This is powerful stuff, and Saunders Lewis has achieved a modern classic with his version, called simply *Siwan*.

VII. Resume A55 east, approaching the impressive cliffs of Penmaen-mawr and skirting them as the road follows the sea-wall. This is a new highway and the signs seem to assume that you are making for Chester; make sure you don't miss the exit on to A470 (signposted to Betws-y-coed). After about 7 miles south down this beautiful Vale of Conwy, look for a driveway going up on the left with the sign 'Hotel Maenan' for a good viewpoint and REST STOP.

Proceed on A470 south to Llanrwst. Park in the parking lot on the right as you enter the town, and walk on the pathway past the toilets and over the stream bridge, to the Parish Church of St Crwst (the Welsh form of St Restitutus). The Gwydir Chapel adjoins the church, with its own doorway.

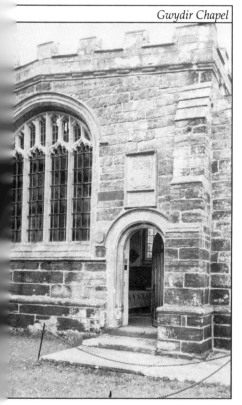

Gwydir Chapel

4.8 The Great Sarcophagus of Gwydir Chapel, Llanrwst

This chapel, built in 1633 (restored in 1965) is said to have been designed by the distinguished Welsh architect Inigo Jones. There are elaborate monuments to the Wynn family; but we are here because it represents the end of the trail for the most notable of the northern princes, Llywelyn the Great, as it houses the large stone coffin which is said to have been his. Llywelyn was buried at the monastery at Aberconwy; then the body was apparently brought to Abaty Maenan, the site of which you may have noticed on the way down, past the Hotel Maenan. Then this coffin or sarcophagus was deposited here at the Dissolution of the monasteries. The provenance is by no means certain, but it has seemed fitting through the years to think that it would take this large a coffin for someone who earned the title 'the Great' by living life up to the hilt. Dafydd Benfras was Llywelyn's bard, and dutifully and, it strikes one, feelingly wrote 'A Lament' at his death.

> Where run the white rolling waves,
> Where meets the sea the mighty river,

In cruel tombs at Aberconwy
God has caused their dire concealment from us,
The red-speared warriors, their nation's illustrious son.

VIII.   The next segment, an hour's detour to William Morgan's birthplace, should be considered optional. The day may be too advanced for such an adventure, and the house closes at dusk. But the National Trust has done a nice job with Tŷ Mawr, and the rewards of this particular countryside are exceptional.

From Llanrwst proceed south on A470 to Betws-y-coed, then take A5 east (towards Llangollen) as far as the junction where B4406 goes off to the right to Penmachno. In this charming village which invites delay you will see signs to Tŷ Mawr erected by the National Trust. Follow the winding road, and further signs, across the Wybrnant Valley, to the remote Tŷ Mawr. Ignore the official car park, and park at the house itself down the hill.

4.9 Tŷ Mawr, Birthplace of William Morgan (1545-1604)

William Morgan, translator of the Welsh Bible, has been seen at work in a previous section (3.4). His revered birthplace has now been restored to the authentic condition of an old-style upland farm cottage. This modest beginning (hardly a *tŷ mawr* 'house big' except in a world of very small houses) boggles the mind: how did the young William Morgan get from remote Snowdonia to St John's College, Cambridge? His father's landlord, Sir John Wynn of Gwydir (whose chapel we have just come from in Llanrwst), must have had something to do with it. There is also the persistent story that William was taught as a youth by a monk who had fled to the seclusion of the Wybrnant valley after the sacking of Maenan Abbey. 'It is attractive,' says Richard Tudor Edwards in his book on William Morgan, 'to imagine the humped sage figure of the monk bending over the boy's papers in this lonely farmhouse, drilling him with the perilous exactness of Greek and Latin. And it is also easy to imagine that boy paying his weekly visits to the great house of Gwydir, under the patronage of the Squire himself.'

> *It is possible to proceed north on the farm road, and with the opening (and closing) of five gates, descend down to the River Lledr. Make a left turn and cross the bridge on to A470, west.*

> *IX.   Those proceeding directly from Llanrwst will also be taking A470 west (towards Blaenau Ffestiniog). The outline of Dolwyddelan Castle will be seen soon after passing the village of that name; the castle car park is on the right side of A470. It is rather a long climb up. Castles are rarely convenient.*

4.10 Dolwyddelan, the Stronghold of the Princes
This was probably the birthplace of Llywelyn the Great (of the Gwydir sarcophagus 4.8), having been built by his father Iorwerth around 1170.

> *Proceeding south on A470 you enter slate-mining country. if you are arriving here before 5 pm you may want to turn in at the well-marked sign on the left of the road to an optional tourst attraction.*

4.11 Llechwedd Slate Caverns
Visitors may take a tram-ride down into the underground quarries of 1846. It is a safe, and well conducted tour. The exhibitions and facilities are exemplary.

> *XI.   There is enough slate to be seen above ground as one drives into Blaenau Ffestiniog on A470, which is your route all the way south through Ffestiniog, Dolgellau, and Dinas*

Mawddwy to Cemaes junction, where A489 west takes you into Machynlleth, and A487 from there into Aberystwyth.

Day 5

Politicians, Preachers, Poets and Patriots

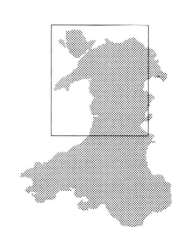

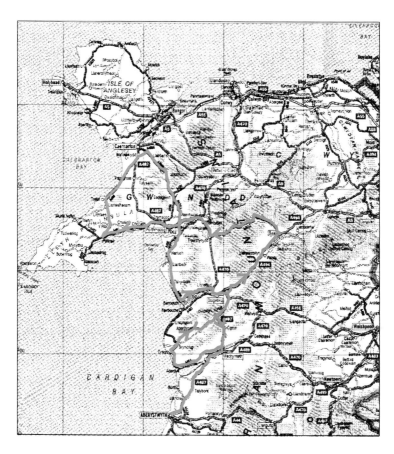

DAY 5: Politicians, Preachers, Poets, and Patriots

We turn north for the final time to visit sites associated with ancient and modern figures revered in the annals of Welsh national history.

I	**From Aberystwyth on A487 – with visit to Gelli-goch (5.1) just before Machynlleth**
II	**Past the Dyfi bridge at Machynlleth, take A493 through Tywyn to Bryn-crug and Mary Jones's grave (5.2)**
III	**Take the unnumbered road signposted to Craig y Deryn to Castell y Bere (5.3) and Mary Jones's cottage beyond Llanfihangel-y-Pennant (5.4)**
IV	**Return to the road to Abergynolwyn, and take B4405 north to A487 north to the cut-off B4416 to A494 – stop at the O.M.Edwards statue at Llanuwchllyn (5.5) and Michael D.Jones's grave at Yr Hen Gapel (5.6)**
V	**Take A494 into Bala – to the Tom Ellis monument (5.7) and that of Thomas Charles (5.8)**
VI	**Out of Bala take A4212 – with a short detour on B4501 for the home of Bob Tai'r Felin (5.9)**
VII	**Take A4212 west up the flooded valley of Tryweryn (5.10)**
VIII	**Continue on A4212 west to Trawsfynydd and the statue of Hedd Wyn (5.11)**

IX	*Take A487 north through Maentwrog and west through Porthmadog; bear left on A497 to Llanystumdwy and the Lloyd George Museum (5.12)*
X	*Take A497 into Pwllheli and the Plaid Cymru plaque (5.13)*
XI	*Out of Pwllheli take A499 east then north towards Caernarfon; at the A487 junction, go north until the unnumbered road to Rhosgadfan and Kate Roberts's cottage (5.14)*
XII	*From Rhosgadfan proceed north on unnumbered road to join A4085. Turn south to Rhyd-ddu and T.H.Parry-Williams's birthplace (5.15)*
XIII	*Continue south on A4085 through Beddgelert to the A487 junction. Cross to the unnumbered toll road to join A496 south – take B4573 to visit Y Lasynys (5.16)*
XIV	*Proceed on B4573 through Harlech – with a visit to Llanfair Church and back to Aberystwyth via Dolgellau.*

I. Take the familiar A487 but just before Machynlleth turn right for a hundred yards into the first road after the village of Derwen-las (signposted Glas-pwll) to see Gelli-goch, the private house on the left-hand side of the road.

5.1 Hugh Williams ('Rebecca') of Gelli-goch, near Machynlleth

It is in keeping with the theme of today's trip, the Welsh striving for self-reliance, that we should begin by paying respects to Hugh Williams (1796-1874) at his birthplace, Gelli-goch, a house of great dignity. Established in his adult life in Carmarthenshire, Williams is supposed to have been the master-mind behind the Rebecca 'Riots' in the mid-nineteenth century, where the farmers were sometimes disguised in women's clothes when they went to pull down the toll-gates. (The text was Genesis 24:60, 'And they blessed Rebekah, and said to her, "Our sister, be the mother of thousands of ten thousands; and may your descendants possess the gate of those who hate

Gelli-goch

them!" ') The secret of Hugh Williams's leadership was well-kept (and Karl Francis in his recent film *Rebecca and her Daughters* promulgates a different view), but he was openly sympathetic. As a solicitor, he defended gratis some of the protesters brought to court. He addressed Chartist meetings, Working Men's Association meetings, and was watched by the police. He compiled an anthology of radical verse, *National Songs and Poetical Pieces,* dedicated to 'the Queen and her countrywomen' perhaps a code for Rebecca and her daughters? (See also **6.10**.)

II. At the Machynlleth clocktower, go straight ahead on A487 across the Afon Dyfi, and take the left fork on A493 through Aberdyfi to Tywyn and to the next village Bryn-crug. Just past the small bridge in the village, turn right on the road signposted to Tal-y-llyn and Craig y Deryn. Park immediately in the car park near the public toilets. Walk the few yards to Bethel Chapel.

5.2 Mary Jones's Grave, Bryn-crug

There is a slate sign at the chapel gate, and the memorial stone is clearly seen to the left as one goes round to the rear of the chapel. There is a new stone as well as an old stone laid flat. The inscription reads: 'In Memory of MARY JONES Who in the Year 1800, At the age of 16, Walked from Llanfihangel-y-Pennant to Bala to procure a copy of a Welsh Bible from Rev Thomas Charles, BA. This incident led to the formation of the British and Foreign Bible Society.' The new monument was erected by the

Bethel, Bryn-crug

members of the Sunday Schools of Merionethshire. There is a slot in the outside of the chapel wall for donations.

89

III. We will now make for Mary Jones's home, and follow her walk, with detours, to Bala.

The desired road begins opposite the parking space; it is the one signposted to Craig y Deryn ('Rock of the Bird'), and it soon gives one a sight of this nature preserve for cormorants, towering to the right as one passes. You may see a signpost to Abergynolwyn on this road, but you will turn off when you see the sign to Llanfihangel, Castell y Bere and Cartref Mary Jones (marked 'dead end'). You will soon see the car park for Castell y Bere on the left. Park and walk to the castle ruins.

5.3 Castell y Bere in the Dysynni Valley

Llywelyn 'the Last' had a younger brother Dafydd who, after Llywelyn's death in 1282, pronounced himself 'Prince of Wales', fought skirmishes against Edward and survived for ten months in defiance. One of the surprising moves he made during this period was the flamboyant gesture of spending three weeks to greet the spring in the Dysynni Valley. Again we are struck by the sheer beauty of the location of a purely Welsh castle. Castell y Bere did not dominate the valley with a military threat; clearly, it was a retreat, chosen for its pleasant air, and the back door escape route across Cader Idris, which Dafydd took when the English forces finally came, no English foot prior to that in this valley. But as you stand on what remains of the old parapet – and quite an impressive amount does – think of the *fin de siècle* atmosphere here, the heady lightness of those three weeks, probably five hundred people enjoying the produce of the fertile Dysynni after the privation of winter in Snowdonia, the yellow flowers flashing out among the dark gorse of the surrounding hills. This was the last self-contained moment of free Wales, 1283.

Not 1282, as the history books for so long led us to believe, casting their gaze away from Dafydd, who was felt to detract from the glory that had always gone to Llywelyn. For instance, Sir John Edward Lloyd's two-volume *A History of Wales* (1911) ends with Llywelyn's death, not Dafydd's. Nationalist historians have dealt unkindly with Dafydd because he fled to England a couple of times and joined forces against his brother. But read the full record and you get a picture of a proud young man, sticking to the old principle of *gavelkind*, i.e. the equal distribution of inheritance among the surviving sons. In order to build a fighting machine, Llywelyn felt he had to take all the power into his own hands; and he has been praised for this; but it is rather un-Welsh, and you can't really expect his brother to have co-operated. The elder brother Owain was imprisoned by Llywelyn in Dolbadarn castle for twenty years; Dafydd was more quick-footed and simply made a nuisance of himself *on principle!* But every act of his, properly interpreted, can be considered that of a patriot, someone well worthy to admire as the last freedom fighter of Wales, 1283.

> *Mary Jones's cottage is just a few hundred yards further on from Castell y Bere, through Llanfihangel-y-Pennant village to the bridge over Afon Cader. On the immediate right, a plaque marks the ruined cottage.*

5.4 Tyn-y-ddôl, Mary Jones's Cottage

The story is a simple one. This is the cottage in which Mary Jones, a weaver's daughter, became imbued with the idea of owning her own Bible. From the age of ten she started saving, and at the end of six years she had three shillings and sixpence. This she took with her on a barefoot journey of twenty-five miles over Cader Idris to Bala. She sought out the famous preacher Thomas Charles, and when she finally gained his presence, he had to tell her that there was no Bible to be bought. The story is that he gave her his own, and that her zeal inspired him to create the British and Foreign Bible Society in order to make free Bibles available to all who wanted them throughout the world. The Bible Mary Jones obtained from Thomas Charles, with her written attestation, was preserved by the Society, and is now in Cambridge University Library.

Look north at the passes over Cader Idris, and you will understand how this story of quiet determination has inspired many besides Thomas Charles.

IV. We cannot follow Mary Jones directly north; we have to retrace our steps back to the turn-off, and then proceed on the road signposted to Abergynolwyn. There we turn left on B4405 (signposted to Dolgellau). As you approach the long lake Tal-y-llyn, be ready to pull left into the shoreline car park of the Penybont Hotel for a REST STOP. (Mary Jones could have stopped here.)

Proceed along the beautiful lake road to join A487 north through a dramatic mountain pass and a straight run to join A470. Turn left and take A470 for about a mile, and look out for B4416 the short-cut through Brithdir off to the right. Pick up A494, turning right to Bala.

Just before Bala Lake comes into sight, at the turn-off to the village of Llanuwchllyn ('Church Above the Lake'), you will see on the right of the highway a double bronze statue of two male figures. Park on the roadside.

5.5 O.M.Edwards of Llanuwchllyn

The two men of the statue, father and son, have been given this recognition for their service to Wales in the area of education, especially in their work for children. O.M.Edwards had, for instance, founded *Cymru'r Plant* ('Wales of the Children'), had edited it, and written most of it, for twenty years up to his death in 1920. There is a nice story of Ifan ab Owen Edwards, carrying on at Oxford after his father's funeral, taking his final exams, and coming home to his lodgings to find a package: it was the proofs of the issue of *Cymru'r Plant* that his father had prepared for the press as one of his last acts. Ifan ap (as he was called – 'Ifan son of') sat down and began correcting the proofs, and carried on the magazine for the next twenty years.

O.M.Edwards was a classic case of the poor farm boy rising to the heights of academic life at Oxford. In 1889 he was appointed Fellow and Tutor in History at Lincoln College, and stayed eighteen years. But all the time he kept in touch with his roots by writing for and editing Welsh language journals. 'His purpose,' Gwynfor Evans has said in *Welsh Nation Builders*, 'was to put Wales and her history in possession of the Welsh people, to give the nation her memory back.' He returned to work in Wales as the country's first inspector of schools, and succeeded in changing the anti-Welshness of the education system. He lived in his native Llanuwchllyn for the rest of his life, playing a strenuous part in local affairs as well as national campaigns. It is an insight into his character that, looking back on a prodigious output of highest quality, he could write in a letter: 'It would have been better if I had done fewer things and done them better.' What a hard taskmaster he was of himself. 'Had he concentrated on fewer things,' writes Hazel Davies in her *Writers of Wales* study, 'his own life would have been more leisurely but the loss to Wales would have been immeasurable.'

O.M. served as Member of Parliament in London for one year, but only one year. He did not seek re-election; when he built his house in Llanuwchllyn he called it Neuadd Wen – he had his own 'Whitehall' in Wales.

> **The house is still in the hands of descendants. To drive by Neuadd Wen, go to the far end of the village and ask anyone.**

From that vantage, you will see the lake and the surrounding countryside, and you will relish O.M.Edwards's passionate vision, expressed in such a passage as the following:

> Our country is alive under our feet, not a deathly grave. Every hill has its history, every district its romance. Each valley is new, each mountain wears its own glory. And for a Welshman no other country can be like this. The Welshman feels that the struggles of his fathers have consecrated every field, and that the muse of his land has sanctified every mountain. And feeling this way makes

him a true citizen.

In quoting this passage, Gwynfor Evans explains what the *gwerin*, the people of the countryside, meant to O.M.Edwards:

> In writing of his country's history, as in everything he did and wrote, his eyes were on the *gwerin*. The glory of the *gwerin* was at the heart of his vision. 'The glory of the Wales of the princes,' he said, 'did not compare with the glory of the Wales of the *gwerin*.' It was of his father and mother and his Sunday School teachers and their like that he thought. Most of them were workers by hand, craftsmen or small farmers like his father. They and their counterparts in the industrial areas were the people who produced writers and musicians, scholars and thinkers, preachers and politicians, in a word the nation's leaders and intellectuals. It was for these, as he had known them in the Llanuwchllyn of his childhood, that he spent his life. He put extensive selections from the Welsh classics in their hands, including the 52 handsome little volumes of *Cyfres y Fil* and *Llyfrau ab Owain*. He was the first to recognise the greatness of Islwyn, publishing two books of his work, the first a volume of 800 pages. All this he did at the cost of his health and money at a critical time in the history of Welsh literature.

The two men of the statue

Hazel Davies concurs: 'He was an incurable romantic in his vision of the perfection of 'y werin' but,' she adds, 'enough of a realist to recognize that, by the end of his life, his magnificent dreams for Wales were only very slowly being realized, and that the battle against prejudice and ignorance would have to be waged anew by each generation.'

His son certainly did his bit on behalf of the following generation. He created the Urdd Gobaith Cymru (League of Youth of Wales) in 1922. In 1928 he personally supervised, with his wife, two hundred boys who accepted an invitation to camp at Llanuwchllyn. He then bought and adapted the mansion Plas Glan-llyn on the shore of the lake as an Urdd youth club. He also created a children's camp at Llangrannog on the Cardiganshire coast. About 14,000 young people used these facilities, both summer and winter; and, being responsible for their own evening entertainment, they developed talents for performance, and the Urdd National Eisteddfod was a natural consequence.

Gwynfor Evans makes an important point here for those who might be suspicious of the word 'nationalism':

> When the Urdd was growing strongly in the 30's there was a powerful youth movement in Germany. The aims and ethos of Hitler Youth was as different from the Welsh movement as Nazism was from Welsh nationalism, as the three-fold pledge of the Urdd indicates: 'I will be faithful to Wales and worthy of her, to my fellow human being whoever he may be and to Christ and his love.' The nationalism of the Welsh movement was Christian and international. Handbooks were published for use in Christian services; an Urdd Sunday was held; and in the month of May each year a Message of Goodwill was broadcast to the countries of the world.

The *Urdd* has now three hundred youth clubs, with 52,000 members and a full-time staff of over fifty. This is why there are two figures memorialized by the common highway at Llanuwchllyn.

> *Go on from the statues a few hundred yards, crossing the bridge over Afon Lliw; take the first road to the left (signposted to Trawsfynydd), and you soon see a solid chapel standing in isolation. Park at the roadside.*

5.6 Michael D.Jones, buried at Yr Hen Gapel

At Yr Hen Gapel ('The Old Chapel') we pay our respects to a great patriot, best known as one of the founders of the Welsh colony in Patagonia. The graves of both Michael D.Jones and his father Michael are near the roadside in the small chapel graveyard. The father was minister here, and Michael D.Jones was born in the chapel house. Educated at home, he knew Latin and Greek at an early age. When he followed his father as Principal of the Congregationalist Bala College, he continued the method of instruction through the medium of

Welsh (the only institute of higher learning doing this at the time), and wrote his own textbook in Welsh for classes in Hebrew. When the great emigrations began in the 1840's, Jones got the idea to put it to advantage rather than let the tide dissipate throughout the world. He formed a commercial company, investing much of his own money. 'Our greatest national weakness today,' he said, 'is our servitude; but in a Welsh settlement our people would possess a new heart and spirit.' The Chubut Valley of Patagonia in the Argentine was decided upon. Although, in the end, only a few thousand actually settled there, it stood for a time as the only independent Welsh political action since the Tudor period. A sum of £2500 was spent on the first venture (out of Michael's wife's dowry, really); when the second try foundered because of the purchase of an unsuitable ship, Jones was forced into bankruptcy. In this emergency, the college bought his house 'Bodiwan' opposite the campus (which we will see shortly) so that he could continue to live there and teach.

Y Wladfa (as the Patagonia colony is called in Welsh) was a great dream, but a hard reality. Its history is summarized in the *Oxford Companion to the Literature of Wales*:

> The first group of Welsh settlers, about 160 in all, mostly from the industrial valleys of south Wales but almost all born in rural districts, set sail from Liverpool on 31 May 1865 on a small ship, *The Mimosa*. Edwin Roberts of Wisconsin and Lewis Jones (1836-1904) led the expedition, but it was Michael D.Jones who provided the political vision and the finance for the enterprise. The party landed on the desolate beach at Porth Madryn on 28 July 1865, celebrated to this day as the Festival of the Landing, and spent several weeks in the shelter of caves. Bitterly disappointed by the wild desert of the Camwy Valley, they endured many years of terrible hardship and would have perished without the practical help in the early days of the Argentinian Government, which sent them food, and of a local tribe of Indians, the Tuelche, who taught them how to hunt. In 1885 a number of families crossed four hundred miles of desert to establish another settlement in Cwm Hyfryd at the foot of the Andes. By the end of the century the settlers had succeeded in controlling the waters of the river Camwy and the valley prospered. Emigration from Wales continued, mostly from the valleys of the south, until 1914.
>
> At the turn of the century Welsh was the language of the colony and all its institutions. Welsh bank-notes were printed, Welsh textbooks were published and Welsh was the language of the

courts. Chapels were built, forming the heart of the colony's cultural life with their prayer-meetings and singing-festivals, and several Welsh newspapers were published, such as *Y Brut* and *Y Drafod*. An annual eisteddfod was held, its competitions giving prominence to the history of the colony, especially as recorded in the diaries describing the pioneers' journey into the heartland. Welsh cultural life began to decline, however, during the first decades of the twentieth century when immigrants from Spain and Italy, attracted by the colony's economic success, began arriving in the province. Contacts with Wales were severed at the start of the Second World War but were restored in 1965 when the colony celebrated its centenary and since then they have continued in a spirit of mutual interest and respect. Only a few of the colony's Welsh-speakers (often bilingual in Welsh and Spanish) have settled in Wales but a number of young Patagonians have spent periods as students in Wales. Even so, Welsh is dying in Patagonia and it is estimated that by today only some five thousand people still speak the language, most of them old or middle-aged. The colony has produced two important Welsh writers, namely Eluned Morgan and R.Bryn Williams.

Michael D.Jones, as his influence spread, was seen as the founder of modern Welsh nationalism. Lloyd George often expressed his debt to Michael D.Jones, as did T.E.Ellis. O.M.Edwards, who had been one of his students in the college, wrote of his inspiration:

> He aroused my interest in Welsh history and taught me to see the glory of those who had struggled for Wales, while at school I was taught to admire those who had injured her. He kindled my zeal, fired my ambition, set a goal before me . . . I got in his company something no school or college ever gave me, – an enlightened love of Wales and her history, and an unshakeable belief in the powerful force which has since been given the name Nationalist . . . For a year he taught me to write Welsh history from a Welsh standpoint . . . In leaving Bodiwan, the old hero's home, I would be determined to do all I could to serve our country and its *gwerin*.

V.   Return to the main road (A494), and take it north along the shore of Llyn Tegid ('Lake Beautiful') into the town of Bala. Park in High Street under the bronze statue of Tom Ellis MP, facing you as you approach.

5.7 Statue of T.E.Ellis MP, Bala

The prominence of this statue in the main thoroughfare is an indication of the high esteem in which Tom Ellis was held by his own people. His dates (1859-1899) tell the story of an early death for a man who 'for six brilliant years,' in the words of Gwynfor Evans, 'was the unquestioned leader of Wales, incorporating the hope of the period's political awakening.' From humble beginnings as the son of a tenant farmer just north of Bala, he rose through the village school, Bala grammar school, University College at Aberystwyth, and New College, Oxford, to become a very effective public speaker. At the early age of 27 he was elected MP on what was essentially a platform of Welsh nationalism. His hero was Charles Stuart Parnell, and he aimed to unify the Welsh Liberal members as Parnell had done the Irish members. He was a better speaker than Parnell, but he lacked one thing: Parnell's financial security as a landowner. Gladstone must have played on this in offering Ellis the prestigious post of Liberal 'Whip' – the job of making sure the MPs keep in line with Government policy. Gwynfor Evans believes that Ellis would not have made the mistake of accepting something that would effectually gag him if it had not been that his health had been dangerously impaired by typhus and diphtheria contracted in Egypt. He was bedridden for ten weeks in 1890, and never fully healthy thereafter. Gwynfor writes of the lost opportunity when the Cymru Fydd movement mushroomed under Lloyd George's leadership after the 1892 election:

> many called on Tom Ellis to cut himself free from the Government in order to lead the movement. Cymru Fydd's peak success was the declaration in Cardiff by Lord Rosebery, the Prime Minister, of his support for a Parliament for Wales. Tom Ellis stayed in the Government however and the movement declined as rapidly as it had risen for a number of reasons but mainly for the lack of Liberal support.

> He worked hard inside the system to help the nationalists to win such important successes as the establishment of the national University and to move towards a national Museum and national Library. As chief guest in the British Empire Club dinner in 1893 he could claim with some justification that, 'At the present time Wales and her people are receiving far more consideration than at any time in their history since their conquest by the Saxons.' But

because the chance of establishing an independent Welsh party had been lost there was no hope of a fundamental improvement in the nation's status.

Time was not given Tom Ellis to rectify his mistake and fulfill his early promise. Some of this pathos must have been in the minds of those who had carved on the pedestal of Tom Ellis's statue the words *Amser Dyn Yw Ei Gynhysgaeth* (literally, 'Time of a Man is his Gift').

5.8 Thomas Charles, Capel Tegid, Bala

Across the street not far down High Street is Thomas Charles's house, now a Barclay's Bank. There is a plaque to remind us that this is the door on which Mary Jones knocked in order to ask for her Bible.

Capel Tegid, where Charles preached so successfully (it seats 1000), is just down Heol Tegid off to the left (east). If his statue, outside the chapel, looks like a Roman senator, that may be because he had influence in his community equivalent to a law-maker. As a scholar Charles had many talents and achievements, but what is counted his greatest achievement was the organisation of a system of Welsh-language Sunday schools. As we have already pointed out, Sunday school in Methodist Wales is quite different from elsewhere: adults as well as children are pupils; it is voluntary, but taken very seriously; rank in society is discounted for this particular hour; the teachers come from all walks of life, and some are university professors; children recite and obtain their best and lasting Welsh here. That these Sunday schools are still a strong element in the weekly life of very many Welsh communities is in a large measure due to their being well founded by Thomas Charles. We should not forget too that it was Thomas Charles who led the Methodists of Wales out of the Church of England, forming their first independent denomination.

> **VI. At the top of High Street, take the left fork A4212 (signposted to Trawsfynydd), and drive slowly up the hill out of Bala. Facing you on the right is the extensive structure of**

Coleg Y Bala, now a Methodist Youth Centre. On the left, obscured somewhat by a wall of trees, is Michael D.Jones's imposing stone house 'Bodiwan'. There is now a plaque with his name and dates and the words:

Arloeswr Rhyddid Cymru
(Pioneer of Freedom of Wales)
Bu fyw yma ym Modiwan.
(He lived here in Bodiwan.)

Proceed along A4212, and make the briefest of detours to the right up B4501 (signposted Cerrigydrudion) for ½ mile to Tai'r Felin farm on the left-hand side of the road. Park by the gate.

5.9 Home of Bob Tai'r Felin

The small roadside plaque portrait of Bob Tai'r Felin ('Bob of the Houses of the Mill') contains the simple words: *'Canwr Cerddi'* i.e. Singer of Songs. Yes, the countryside of Wales is rich with many singers of song. Bob Tai'r Felin was outstanding. Gwynfor Evans speaks of him as 'the cultured old farmer and ballad-singer, whose tenor voice rang out like a bell, even at eighty years of age.' The plaque indicates how much this is appreciated in Wales.

VII. Returning to A4212, turn right and continue west and you will soon come to what on recent maps is named Llyn Celyn, though everybody knows that it is not really a lake but a reservoir. Pull in to the first parking bay past the damsite parking itself.

5.10 The Flooded Valley of Tryweryn

On a rock that you will see in this parking bay is a plaque which reads:

Under these waters and near this stone stood Hafod Fadog, a farmstead where in the seventeenth and the eighteenth centuries

Quakers met for worship. On the hillside above the house was a space encircled by a low stone wall, where larger meetings were held, and beyond the house was a small burial ground. From this valley came many of the early Quakers who emigrated to Pennsylvania, driven from their homes by persecution to seek freedom of worship in the New World.

On the tarmac below the rock is painted in broad yellow letters:

'LIVERPOOL'S SHAME'

'Remember Tryweryn' was one of the great rallying cries of the Welsh nationalist movement in the fifties and sixties. Liverpool was planning to destroy a living community in Wales, not for any necessity but because it had bought the legal right to do so. Plaid Cymru took the fight right into the Liverpool City Council Chambers, where Gwynfor Evans offered a scheme whereby Liverpool could get all the water it wanted from the valley of a tributary of the Tryweryn without drowning a single home. The whole of the doomed village of Capel Celyn marched through the streets of the city. The campaign won the support of almost the whole of Wales. All the Welsh MP's in Westminster, except one, voted against the Bill to allow Liverpool to go ahead, but it passed in the House of Commons by 175 votes to 79 during the summer of 1957. Such things are remembered.

Some small satisfaction was gained from the fact that the Opening Ceremony in October 1965 did not go quite according to plan. This is how Gwynfor describes it in *Fighting For Wales:*

At the foot of the huge dam a colourful canvas pavilion had been erected to accommodate a host of distinguished guests and civic dignitaries invited to celebrate the opening of the enormous lake. A buffet lunch had been prepared in the pavilion. When their cavalcades of cars arrived the welcome in the hillsides was not to their liking. Some five hundred nationalists had gathered to greet them with jeers rather than joy, and when they assembled in the pavilion the tumult was so great that few distinguished guests could hear a word from the platform. In a few minutes there were no words to be heard. Welsh anger burst forth in a charge of hundreds down the steep slope to the pavilion. The wires of the public address system were severed. The Lord Mayor could be seen opening and shutting his mouth but no sound came forth. His voice was drowned in uproar and soon he ceased trying to speak. Some ropes were cut and part of the pavilion collapsed, doing no

physical injury but effectively terminating the ceremony.
Liverpool's bright morning ended in a shambles, engulfed by the
wrath of Wales.

Although the Tryweryn campaign did not significantly
strengthen the national party in Merioneth, where I was the Plaid
Cymru candidate, it made a deep and lasting impression on the
industrial valleys of Glamorgan and Gwent and on people in their
teens in all parts of Wales. Some of the present leaders of Plaid
Cymru have said that it was the Tryweryn campaign that
awakened their national spirit.

At a parking bay further on (without, however, a signpost
of any kind) there is the entrance to a newly built structure
down by the water. The following explanation can be found on
the doorway: 'This building together with the Garden of
Remembrance was erected as a Memorial for the Chapel and
Burial Ground of Capel Celyn now submerged by Llyn Celyn.'
With the added note: 'Key is Available at Power House.' At the
back of the new 'chapel' are the gravestones gathered from the
old graveyard of Capel Celyn.

> VIII. Continue on A4212 west, a new road built since the dam,
> to Trawsfynydd, and follow the sign to the town centre, where
> there is parking at the Medical Building adjacent to the public
> toilets. Walk to the prominent statue on the main street by the
> chapel Eglwys Moriah.

5.11 Statue of Hedd Wyn, Trawsfynydd

'Hedd Wyn' ('Peace White') was the bardic name chosen by a
self-educated farm lad of this district called Ellis Humphrey
Evans, whose joy was competing in the eisteddfodau. The old
Shell Guide suggests the name came from 'the white peace of
the mists that hang about these hills, and that were so much
the companions of his daily life.' When the First World War
came with its poison gas, the name became pathetically ironic.
Hedd Wyn enlisted with the Royal Welsh Fusiliers early in
1917 at the age of thirty; he was killed on 31 July. The National
Eisteddfod of Wales was held in September at Birkenhead and
the winning poet was called to take his Chair. It was Hedd

Hedd Wyn

Wyn, and he could not reply to the summons. People still speak today with emotion about the empty chair on the stage,
which was draped with a black cloth. The statue that you see here, however, portrays Hedd Wyn idealistically and ever young, with the rolled-up sleeves and gaitered trousers of a shepherd boy.

IX. Go north through the village to join A487 north through Maentwrog and, still on A487, west to Porthmadog.

There is a toll collected at 'The Cob', the mile-long embankment carrying the road and the Ffestiniog narrow-gauge railway across the former great marsh of Traeth Mawr. It is a quaint reminder of the toll-gates of previous times, which caused real suffering at this spot. Perhaps a symbolic non-payment is in order, though 'Rebecca' never operated this far north.

Through the resort town of Porthmadog, take the left fork A497. When this road reaches the sea, you will see Criceth and, beautiful from a distance, its castle, a seaside villa of the Welsh princes. Continue 1½ miles to Llanystumdwy and take the old road into the village. Pull in to the car park of the Feathers Hotel for a REST STOP. Or proceed a few yards further and (right) into the well-signalled 'Lloyd George Museum'.

5.12 Lloyd George Museum, Llanystumdwy

The most famous Welshman of all time, prime minister of Great Britain during the First World War and after, needs no introduction. There is a video presentation inside the Museum for those who want to experience his life. What is not usually stressed is how much of a Welsh Nationalist Lloyd George was in his pre-cabinet days. As we have noted, Michael D.Jones was a deep influence, and Tom Ellis was a comrade in arms. Lloyd George continued to fight for Cymru Fydd ('Wales of the Future') after Tom Ellis was neutralized. He campaigned in the Welsh-speaking valleys of Glamorgan and Gwent, purporting to be giving a lecture on Llywelyn the Great. 'I am sure,' he is quoted as saying, 'that if it achieved self-government Wales would be an example to the countries of the world.' Then this movement, for one reason or another, collapsed, and Lloyd George went on to use his immense talents for self-promotion. He was, of course, so successful in this that he gained the ultimated height from which he could send millions to their death, like Hedd Wyn on Pilken Ridge on 31 July 1917.

As an elder statesman of seventy-three he ridiculed the fledgling Welsh Nationalist Pary from the platform of the 1936 Fishguard Eisteddfod; but soon after that came Penrhos Aerodrome, the symbolic act of arson by the pacifist leaders of Plaid Cymru, and Lloyd George had a change of heart somewhat. After the authorities failed to get the arsonists convicted by a Welsh jury and started a second trial in London, he wrote the following in a letter to his daughter about the Chamberlain government:

> They yield when faced by Hitler and Mussolini, but they attack the smallest country in the kingdom which they misgovern . . . This is the first government that has tried to put Wales on trial in the Old Bailey . . . I should like to be there, and I should like to be forty years younger.

Lloyd George's grave is in a peaceful glade by the banks of Afon Dwyfor. Walk back through the 'Victorian Garden' to Highgate Cottage, furnished for tourists as it was when Lloyd

George was brought up there by his shoemaker uncle in the 1860's.

X. Leave Llanystumdwy by the road west and pick up A497 west to Pwllheli. Once in the town, follow the signs to A497 (towards Nefyn) and park in the free public parking by the Tourist Information office and public toilets.

5.13 Plaid Cymru Plaque, Maes, Pwllheli

The Maesgwyn Temperance Hotel no longer exists. The building is now occupied by 'Edwards Ellis, Pet and Garden Centre'. A plaque, however, can be seen above the door:

Yma	[Here
Mewn Cyfarfod A Gynhaliwyd	In a meeting that was held
Ar Awst 5, 1925	on August 5, 1925
Y Sefydlwyd	was founded
Plaid Genedlaethol Cymru	Party National of Wales]

On that day in what was an upstairs room of the hotel, six people met: Saunders Lewis and Fred Jones from South Wales, and Lewis Valentine, Moses Griffith, H.R.Jones and David Edmund Williams from North Wales. The decision there was to launch a nationalist party for Wales, Plaid Cymru, with a Summer School to be held the following year at Machynlleth (as the site of Owain Glyndŵr's Parliament) and an all-Welsh newspaper *Y Ddraig Goch* ('The Red Dragon') inaugurated. Events of significance cannot always secure their proper visible memorial. The Pwllheli Bus Station bustling with English holiday-makers from the near-by Starcoast World (formerly Butlin's Holiday Camp) is not quite the desired ambience for meditating on the founding of the Welsh Nationalist Party in a place which is now a pet shop, with the Conservative Club next door, and a 'Mr Cheep' outlet on the other side. Wales, as one of its illustrious visitors Leopold Kohr would say, cries out for a desirable smallness of scale. The elbowing and bulging of crass consumerism has no place, any more than the low-flying aircraft of the RAF, who might be breaking the sound barrier over your head at any time on this Llŷn Peninsula.

Which brings us to the Penrhos Aerodrome affair. In 1936 Penyberth, a few miles west of Pwllheli, was chosen by Westminster for a new RAF Bombing School — after proposals for other sites in England had been defeated by local inhabitants. Plaid Cymru marshalled the instinctive revulsion in Wales to this alien idea and sent a protest letter to Prime Minister Baldwin with the names of one thousand representative bodies in Wales objecting to the Penyberth site. But the plan went ahead, and bulldozers demolished the beautiful old farmhouse of Penyberth and started work on what was to have been called Penrhos Aerodrome. At 1.30 am on 8 September 1936, Saunders Lewis, a university lecturer, Lewis Valentine, a Baptist minister, and D.J.Williams, a teacher and writer, set fire to timber stored in the compound; then gave themselves up at the Pwllheli police station. The protest made an enormous impact. The Caernarfon Court was surrounded by crowds through the trial of the three. Saunders Lewis was brilliant in turning the case against the English government, and the jury refused to convict. With a hung jury, the authorities transferred the case to the Old Bailey in London, with all the bitter reaction – Lloyd George's we have already quoted (5.12). The Plaid leaders were given a nine-month sentence in Wormwood Scrubs prison, but the Welsh nationalist spirits had never been higher.

It is difficult today to find the exact spot where this 'Fire in Llŷn' took place. There is a signpost to Penyberth along A499 west (towards Aber-soch), but of course the house of that name was destroyed in 1936, and the RAF camp is now a caravan site. This is not a journey of homage that can be recommended. (I am told that there is a plaque somewhere, but I have on two visits been unable to find it.)

XI.   Circle back through Pwllheli on A499 east and continue on A499 north (towards Caernarfon). The twin peaks of Yr Eifl ('The Forks') will rise on your left. On reaching the sea past Clynnog Fawr, you will see the coastline and island named on some maps as Maen Dylan.

This is the point on the coast where it is said that Dylan Eil Ton ('Dylan Son of Wave') was born, and immediately sought the sea 'and took its nature, and swam as well as the best fish that was therein' (according to the Mabinogi*). The name given to Dylan Thomas by his parents, rare at the time, is said to have come from this story (there also happened to be an Opera entitled 'Dylan' performed in Swansea the year Dylan was born).*

When A499 reaches the junction with A487, turn left (towards Caernarfon) and take A487 north for about a mile until you see an unnumbered road off to the right signposted to Rhosgadfan, and climb up to that village. Park when you see the Rhosgadfan football field and clubhouse, and the small ruined cottage nearby.

5.14 Kate Roberts's Cottage, Rhosgadfan

Hen Gartref Kate Roberts
Y Nofelydd
Y Lôn Wen
Ffair Gaeaf
O Gors y Bryniau
Laura Jones
Deian a Loli
Rhigolau Bywyd
Te yn y Grug
Traed Mewn Cyffion

The plaque on the cottage 'Cae'r Gors', where Wales's foremost novelist of recent times was born and brought up,

Kate Roberts (1891-1985), lists her eight chief works of fiction. For an assessment of this lifetime of work, all in Welsh (though some is translated), we turn to Derec Llwyd Morgan's critique in the *Writers of Wales* series:

> Kate Roberts's imaginative world is composed of two distinct layers of life. The first, lower layer contains a sad picture of the life of a slate-quarrying community in Arfon . . . From 1935 until her death she lived in Denbigh, and thus knew at first hand the somewhat neurotic contemporary small-town life of north Wales contained in her second layer of literature . . . Her world is authentically hers; she was above all things a creator of people, solid, articulate, sensitive people who move and breathe in a land she depicted for their habitation. Her mastery of idiom and syntax was renowned, few of her fellows matched her sensitivity, and the people of her books are so nervously alive that one feels a social historian attempting a description of Edwardian Arfon or mid-twentieth century Denbigh would be inevitably vain if he did not begin his work with an analysis of Kate Roberts's stories, for the characters there and the situations she invented possess the authoritative truth only the genius of imagination can produce.

Readers who have no Welsh might get from the library a small selection of Kate Roberts's short stories in translation, entitled *A Summer Day* (1946). Two novels, *The Living Sleep* and *Feet in Chains* have been available in Corgi paperback since 1981. We now have the benefit of a comprehensive collection,

Kate Roberts's cottage

The World of Kate Roberts: Selected Stories 1925-1981, translated and edited by Joseph P.Clancy, published by Temple University in Philadelphia (1991), distributed by the University of Wales Press. This volume may be, finally, enough to create the interest that this world-class writer deserves in the world at large. In Wales she has had great renown and regard not only as a novelist but as a nationalist. Kate Roberts was a member of Plaid Cymru from the earliest days, contributing regularly to *Y Ddraig Goch*. With her husband she ran the publishing house Gwasg Gee in Denbigh, and edited the newspaper *Baner ac Amserau Cymru*, a great forum for debate on Welsh questions.

At the top of the list of Kate Roberts's novels on the plaque is *Y Lôn Wen* ('The Lane Blessed'). Unfortunately this work has not yet been translated, but we can drive along the actual 'lane' and see the view which, as the plaque there says, 'has refreshed the spirit of many and inspired the writings of Kate Roberts of Rhosgadfan.'

> **Go up a few more yards to the top road of the village (at the post office), turn left on to a road that stretches out north onto the moorland. After about ½ mile, you will see on the left a low-walled enclosure in which you may park, read the plaque, and look at the view therein described.**

> **XII. Proceed north and east on the moorland road down into Gwyrfai Valley, meeting A4085; turn right and drive south, passing Llyn Cwellyn, to Rhyd-ddu. At the south end of the village, look out for the old stone school on the right, and turn into the car park behind it.**

5.15 T.H.Parry-Williams's School House, Rhyd-ddu

We come here to pay respects to the man pre-eminent among twentieth century poets and scholars. T.H.Parry-Williams's father was headmaster of this primary school, and the plaque on the school house 'Tŷ'r Ysgol' indicates that the poet was born at home, though it goes on to say: '*Mae darnau ohonof ar wasgar hyd y fro*' ('There are fragments of me scattered through the homeland'). T.H.Parry-Williams worked entirely in Welsh, of course, so again we rely on the authority of an expert. R.Gerallt Jones begins his study in the *Writers of Wales* series with the following peroration, which takes its imagery, as the

poet himself so often did, from the landscape you can see
behind the school house at Rhyd-ddu:

> There is a towering symmetry about the life and work of
> T.H.Parry-Williams. One approaches it almost with a sense of
> observing a natural phenomenon. One sees in it the huge,
> inexorable stamina of a glacier. It is awe-inspiring. And yet it is
> also all of a piece. One is struck, as one looks at it, by the rightness
> of things. This, in a sense, is paradoxical. For much of the content
> of his art, in both prose and verse, probes deeply into facets of
> human existence that seem to him to be anything but right. But the
> art itself, measured, structured, fashioned in granite, classically
> restrained to a degree unimagined by his romantic contemporaries,
> makes the only kind of sense that is possible. His writing – with
> him prose and verse are one – is his attempt to clothe the brutish,
> foolish, sad and hilarious realities of human existence with some
> semblance of dignity. Even, at times, with grace. And always with
> the cardinal virtues of courage and intellectual integrity.

There is a photographic biography of T.H.Parry-Williams in
the *Bro a Bywyd* series (1981); the pictures tell the story of
thepoet's precocious triumphs at the eisteddfodau, his
education at Jesus College, Oxford, his career at the University
College at Aberystwyth, his travels to South America in 1925,
and so on. The inner life is in the poetry. Its source is here at
Rhyd-ddu, where the vastness of the mountains forced an
attachment to the warmth of home life. In the famous sonnet
'Moelni', R.Gerallt Jones explains, the smooth contours of the
mountains ('as though giants had been polishing the slopes')
pressed in upon the poet during his childhood until they
became a part of his being. Another sonnet 'Tynfa' expresses a
similar feeling about the River Gwyrfai, which runs through
the village:

> *Os ydyw Afon Gwyrfai wedi troi*
> *Düwch ei dyfroedd trwy fy ngwaedlif i . . .*
>
> (If the River Gwyrfai has diverted
> the course of its dark waters into my bloodstream . . .)

And in 'Sialens', the poet fights against the imminent incursion
of middle-age with thoughts of diminished sensitivity and
passion:

> *Gwae fi o'm tynged, oni ddringaf i*
> *I ben y clogwyn draw a dodi llef*
> *Yn erbyn yr ysbeilwyr*

(Let my fate be cursed, unless I climb
to the head of that crag there and cry out
against these vandals)

> *dof yn ieuanc rydd*
> *Mi wn, o'r sgarmes fawr, pan ddêl ei dydd.*

(I shall emerge young and free,
I know, from that great battle, when the day comes.)

R.Gerallt Jones has called this 'a rare piece of stark, optimistic realism in some ways paralleled by Dylan Thomas's 'rage, rage, against the dying of the light'.' And we see too that this gruffest-looking of all poets was a patriot of Wales in somewhat the same way as Wordsworth was of the Lake District. His famous poem 'Hon', which has been published as a poster that can still be purchased at Siop y Pethe, jabs at the 'prattling of unit and nation', but Snowdonia gives meaning to patriotism:

> And I feel the claws of Wales tearing at my heart.
> God help me I cannot get away from this spot.

This is obviously one of the honest poets of the world:

> *Weithiau – mewn breuddwyd – daw fflach o'r gwir,*
> *Ond wedyn anwiredd a thwyllo hir.*

(Sometimes – in a dream – comes a flash of truth,
but then untruth and long deceit.)

It is to read T.H.Parry-Williams in the original Welsh that one might find oneself beginning the arduous process of learning this language, which is so unfamiliar because neither Germanic nor Romance, though the easeful adoption of borrowed words (such as 'fflach' above) helps.

Back in the village of Rhyd-ddu there is a good inn, the Cwellyn Arms, with food and outside tables. The grocery store on the main thoroughfare is a pleasant place to buy refreshments for a quick REST STOP.

XIII. Continue south on A4085 through Beddgelert to the junction with A487. Cross the highway to the unnumbered road straight ahead, a small toll-road by the railway track across the Afon Dwyryd. This joins A496 south, towards Harlech, but take

it for only about two miles, and past Talsarnau look for a fork left on to B4573 (which used to be the main route to Harlech). After just over a mile, begin to look across the fields on the right of the road for a complex of old buildings of an isolated farm. The entrance gate is opposite a white house on the left; turn right, and take the grass grown farm track to the ruined house.

5.16 Ellis Wynne (1671-1734) and the Ruin of Y Lasynys

By the time you read these words, this birthplace of Ellis Wynne may no longer be in ruins, as restoration has begun. Ellis Wynne is revered for one work of great appeal in its time, *Gweledigaetheu y Bardd Cwsc* ('The Visions of the Sleeping Bard') published in 1703. It is a cross between Milton and Bunyan, with a specific source in the Spanish work of Don Francisco Gomez de Quevedo Villegas. It is not something that would inspire most people to learn Welsh, yet there were five editions in the eighteenth century and twelve editions in the nineteenth. George Borrow translated it in 1860; T.Gwynn Jones did one for the Gregynog Press in 1940. I value the lines 'To the Reader':

Who read, let them ponder;
Who ponder, let them bear in mind;
Who bear in mind, let them do;
Who do, let them hold them fast.

Y Lasynys

The 'sleeping bard' was widely read, but his house, when it ceased to be an active farm, was allowed to go to ruin, until recently. Your presence at this spot may help to speed the process of restoration of the place and the writer's repute.

Ellis Wynne was an ordained clergyman, and had the living at Llanfair, a village south of Harlech, from 1705 until his death. He is buried in the church, a pretty church with easy access from the road, but not usually open.

XIV. Proceed through Harlech with its famous well-preserved non-Welsh Edwardian castle, joining A496 south. To visit Llanfair Church, leave the main road briefly and enter the village. Proceed on A496 through Barmouth and along the exquisitely beautiful Mawddach estuary (see Introduction, above). If you have time, go into the centre of Dolgellau for a supper REST STOP at the Black Lion Inn, and enjoy Eldon Square and the darkened stone of the houses in one of Wales's best towns. Take the usual A487 south through Machynlleth to Aberystwyth.

Day 6

Gwynfor's Country

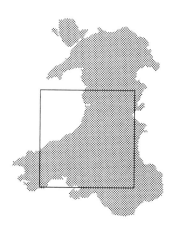

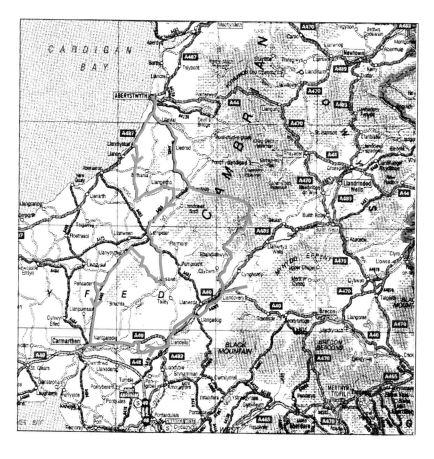

DAY 6: Gwynfor's Country

The present guide is based on the historical books of Gwynfor Evans, Land of My Fathers *and others. This day we visit the parts of Wales where Gwynfor chose to live and fight his main political battles as leader of Plaid Cymru.*

I **Take A487 south from Aberystwyth; left turn on B4337 down to Tal-sarn; left on B4342, and left again on B4576 to Daniel Rowland's birthplace (6.1) then from Bwlch-llan on unnumbered road east to join B4342 to Daniel Rowland's statue in Llangeitho (6.1)**

II **From Llangeitho, proceed east on B4342; turn right on B4578 to join A485 through Llanbedr Pont Steffan; turn east on A482 (towards Llanwrda); after four miles turn right on unnumbered road to Esgairdawe entering D.J.Williams's 'square mile' (6.2). At Llansawel, turn right on B4337 to Gwenallt's Rhydcymerau (6.3)**

III **Proceed west on B4337; turn right on unnumbered road (signposted to Parc-y-rhos) and climb to the Pencarreg Television Transmitter (6.4)**

IV **Return straight down the hill to Pencarreg and find the Red Dragon on the Lawn (6.5)**

V **Proceed on A485 south to the unnumbered road right, signposted to Pencader for the plaque (6.6)**

VI **From Pencader go south on B4459 to rejoin A485, which joins A40 just before Carmarthen – find the Guildhall (6.7)**

VII	Take A40 east out of Carmarthen to Abergwili – stop at the Bishop's Palace (6.8)
VIII	Proceed on A40 east, turn right at B4297 for Dryslwyn Castle on the Afon Tywi (6.9)
IX	Proceed across the river and turn left on B4300 east, which joins A476, which joins A483 into Llandeilo. Leave on A40 – turn on to the unnumbered road to Cwmifor (6.10) continuing to the toll-house and the right turn down to junction with A40. Cross the Afon Tywi on A4069 into Llangadog
X	Take A4069 to Llandovery, and A40 east to the unnumbered road (signposted to Babel), turn left to Pantycelyn (6.11) – retrace steps to A40 and into Llandovery; take A483 and turn off left at the Llanfair-ar-y-bryn Parish Church and the William Williams Pantycelyn monument (6.12)
XI	Back on A483, take the immediate right on the unnumbered road to Rhandir-mwyn, and on to Llyn Brianne Reservoir (6.13)
XII	Take the road east of the reservoir, and follow it to the drover's road into Tregaron and the statue of Henry Richard (6.14)
XIII	Take A485 west, joining A487 just before Aberystwyth.

> *I. Take A487 south from Aberystwyth as far as Llanrhystud, then take the left turn on B4337 down to the junction at Talsarn, turning left on B4343. At about 2 miles look for the signpost to Bwlch-llan, and turn left on B4576. You come first to the parish church of Nantcwnlle on the left of the road, where Daniel Rowland had his first curateship. Proceed to the village centre, and continue on the unnumbered road east (towards Llangeitho). The first farmhouse on the right past the cemetery is Rowland's birthplace, Pantybeudy. Continue on the unnumbered road east to join B4342 again, and into Llangeitho, and immediate left to the Daniel Rowland statue.*

6.1 Daniel Rowland (1713-1790) of Bwlch-llan and Llangeitho

A statue of Daniel Rowland now stands in the grounds of the present chapel in Llangeitho. But no buildings from his day are preserved – and in any case his audiences of up to two thousand would be out in the open air, and that was where he preached, receiving the censure of his superiors in the established church. He never rose above a curate, because he believed in preaching in the open to all-comers. Gwynfor Evans reminds us that Rowland started his preaching mission in 1735; that was three years before John Wesley and four years before George Whitfield: 'Although the Welsh evangelists co-operated with George Whitfield, the revival in Wales was wholly independent of the Methodism of England, both in its origins and its history.' As a

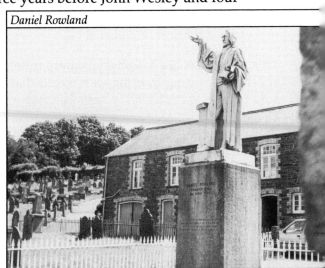

Daniel Rowland

translator of John Bunyan's *Holy War*, his visage as we see it on this statue and in a well-known portrait is appropriately grim. His severe looks while preaching are said to have terrified people out of their carefree way of living and wrought in them a deep sense of sin. This is very believable; what is not so believable is that he changed his stern, reproving manner in his later years, but apparently he did, the sectarian rivalries muted and the sense of sin turning into a sense of holiness.

II. We now make as directly as possible for D.J.Williams's 'square mile'; but this is deep in the countryside of Carmarthenshire, and it is impossible to be very direct.

From Llangeitho, proceed east on B4342, to the junction with B4578; turn right and go south on B4578 to join A485 south through Llanbedr Pont Steffan (Lampeter). Turn off A485 after Llanbedr Pont Steffan, where A482 goes east (signposted Llandovery). At the fourth milestone on A482 there is a cross-roads, where the road to the right is signposted to Esgairdawe. Past Esgairdawe, looking south-west across Afon Marlais, you begin to see 'y filltir sgwâr ('the mile square'), where D.J.Williams had his origins and which he brought to life in his writings. The family farmhouse Pen-rhiw cannot itself be seen from any accessible point.

6.2 D.J.Williams's 'Square Mile'

This, of course, is a visionary 'square mile', full of memories of childhood and aspirations for a world that can be like his small, close community, where, in the words of the *Oxford Companion to the Literature of Wales,* 'human values exalted the individual and the spirit of co-operation was a natural instinct.' Williams left Pen-rhiw at the age of six for Aber-nant near Rhydcymerau, and left there at sixteen for a colliery in the Rhondda. Thence, after eight years, to Aberystwyth and Jesus College, Oxford. But he returned many times; and in depth in his writings. The autobiography that covers the earliest period can sometimes be found in secondhand bookstores in Wales: *The Old Farmhouse* (1961), translated by Waldo Williams, himself an important writer (see 7.11). It is a steady, quietly happy book, and indicates the inner security which allowed D.J. to follow, without the least faltering, the path he thought to be right.

This path, as we have seen (5.13), led him to be an early member of Plaid Cymru and one of the three to do the symbolic arson at Penrhos Aerodrome; this while being a teacher at Abergwaun (Fishguard) County School. As the editors of *Profiles* testify, bare biographical details 'give no indication of the uniqueness of "D.J." ':

> To a stranger he might have seemed a character – almost a caricature – with his round, glistening face, and his pig-like eyes behind their hornrimmed spectacles. He was always the centre of attraction in a crowd, always smiling and causing a smile to ripple through his listeners. In some way he belonged to a different world from that of the youngsters who crowded around him, a survivor from a simpler and purer age, almost a figure from a naïve painting.
>
> D.J. was far from being naïve, however, as those who knew him testify, but he had a singleness of purpose rare among those who regard themselves as sophisticated or cosmopolitan. His utter lack of duplicity, his guilelessness, were such as to make a verbal characterization appear fatuous. One is tempted to say that he was brimming with Welshness. His patriotism seemed an innate quality – not something acquired under persuasion. Since he was one of the 'founding fathers' of the Welsh Nationalist Party in 1925, and an intrepid but cheerful campaigner for the party until the last moments of his life, one immediately thinks of him as a politician, but somehow the label seems out of place. Politics can be – and often is – a dirty business, but not even the enemies of Plaid Cymru could accuse D.J. of playing a political game. His enthusiasm was catching. He was the kind of person who could sell party literature or squeeze financial contributions from tight-fisted strangers of ambiguous persuasion. And he was not a man to seek the limelight. No ordinary day-to-day task was beneath him. Indeed he revelled in canvassing, in addressing envelopes, writing letters, winning new subscribers to the party newspapers, as well as speaking – with persuasive humanity – on countless platforms. One moment of glory – and humiliation – stand out. He was the accomplice of Saunders Lewis and Lewis Valentine in setting fire to the RAF Bombing School at Penyberth near Pwllheli in the Llŷn Peninsula in 1936 – the first example of direct action taken in the cause of Welsh nationalism in modern times. But a hero's mantle does not somehow fit him: when the time came to commit the

'criminal' act of arson, he found that his matches were damp.

After his retirement from teaching in 1945, the last decades of his life were all devoted to Plaid Cymru. When the party needed a new headquarters, he sold his birthright, the house at Pen-rhiw, and gave the money towards it, so the name lives on as the new house name in Carmarthen. His last act at the age of eighty-four was a fund-raising speech for the Rhydaman Eisteddfod back at his old chapel at Rhydcymerau. As Gwynfor has described it, D.J. took the platform, was funny for ten minutes and serious for ten minutes; he pointed at the individual pews, naming all the people who had had them when he was a boy; made his pitch for money; then sat down, and within two minutes collapsed. Gwynfor wrapped his raincoat about him, and he died in his arms. Hundreds came to Gwynfor's house, Talar Wen, where D.J. lay 'in state'. A cortège then brought him back to be buried in the graveyard at Rhydcymerau. In following the trail for this guide, I myself spoke to a resident, Jim Jones Cwmhywel, who remembered that day. D.J. dropped by the farm on his way to the chapel: 'I've given your ewes some water,' he said. Jim Jones described him to me as 'like a ten year old – as though something good was going to happen.'

> **To complete the journey to Rhydcymerau, take the road all the way down to Llansawel, make a right turn, and take B4337 towards Llanybydder. D.J.'s home 'Aber-nant' is down on the left side of the road, and bears a plaque. The graveyard is at the back of the chapel in the centre of the village of Rhydcymerau.**

6.3 Gwenallt's Rhydcymerau

There is another person of renown connected with this place. Though he was born in the Swansea Valley among the steel and tin-plate works (which engendered his strong Marxist beliefs), David James Jones, better known by his bardic name 'Gwenallt', had many relatives in this neighbourhood

(D.J.Williams was one), and often visited the countryside. During the first World War, Gwenallt was a conscientious objector, imprisoned for a period. He became a student at Aberystwyth after the war, and later taught in the Welsh Department there. He won many honours for his poetry, which was angry at times, but mainly tinged with sadness. We can cite his poem 'Rhydcymerau', a protest against the Forestry Commission's planting conifers on the Welsh uplands, creating an unnatural landscape on farmland that capitalist economics has made defunct.

Ac erbyn hyn nid oes yno ond coed,
A'u gwreiddiau haerllug yn sugno'r hen bridd:
Coed lle bu cymdogaeth,
Fforest lle bu ffermydd,
Bratiaith Saeson y De lle bu barddoni a diwinydda,
Cyfarth cadnoid lle bu cri plant ac ŵyn.
Ac yn y tywyllwch yn ei chanol hi
Y mae ffau'r Minotawros Seisnig;
Ac ar golfenni, fel ar groesau,
Ysgerbydau beirdd, blaenoriaid, gweinidogion ac athrawon
    Ysgol Sul
Yn gwynnu yn yr haul,
Ac yn cael eu golchi gan y glaw a'u sychu gan y gwynt.

And by this time there are only trees,
their impudent roots sucking the old earth;
trees where once there was neighbourhood,
a forest where there were farms,
the lingo of the English-speakers of the South
where once was poetry and divinity,
the barking of foxes where once was the cry of children and
    lambs,
and in the darkness in the middle of it
the lair of the English Minotaur;
and on the branches, as though on crosses,
skeletons of poets, deacons, ministers and Sunday school teachers
whitening in the sun,
washed by the rain and dried by the wind.

As we move out west from Rhydcymerau we can see such areas of 'spoilage', the deep green of the non-native trees going up to the horizon on the left; and when we make our turn-off, the road we take will have the dark foreboding work of the Forestry Commission on one side of the road, and the gentle grazing lands of Wenallt Farm on the other. This contrast will be all the more intense when the time comes to harvest these forests by 'clear cut' methods that leave a desolate landscape in their wake.

> **III. Proceed west on B4337; at about 2 miles, look for an unnumbered road to the right signposted to Parc-y-rhos; turn right and climb, making for the television transmission tower that can be seen as a high silhouette in the distance. Bear left at the first junction, then at the next turn sharp right on to a less used road which leads up to the television transmission compound, and car park.**

6.4 The Pencarreg Television Transmitter

The view of four counties from this peak of Pencarreg is extraordinary on a fine day; but we are here to remember a particular event. At 9 pm on 11 November 1979 the television signal from this transmitting station went black. The police found at the scene of the crime Dr Pennar Davies, Principal of Swansea Theological College and a poet; Dr Meredydd Evans, a Senior Lecturer in the Extra-Mural Department of the University College, Cardiff, a well-known folk-singer and authority on Welsh folksong; and Mr Ned Thomas, a Senior Lecturer in English at the University College, Aberystwyth, an editor and television critic. They handed the police a statement that began: 'We have taken this step of switching off the transmitter at Pencarreg in order to focus attention on the worsening crisis in Welsh broadcasting.' This act of disobedience had been preceded by many others, mainly the refusal on the part of hundreds of Welsh families to pay their television licence fees. This pulling of the switch by 'the Pencarreg Three' (as they came to be called) was an escalation; and there was much publicity when the three had their day in court and were, in the end, fined £500 each plus £500 costs. The courtroom speeches were published in a booklet, *The Pencarreg Three.* When Gwynfor Evans wrote in my copy at my request, he wrote: 'In Ned, Pennar and Mered one sees Cymru at its best. Their heroic act at Pencarreg contributed substantially to the Welsh television victory without which the survival of the Welsh language would be far more uncertain.'

> **IV. Retrace your steps on the dirt road, but at the junction keep going straight down the hill into the village of Pencarreg. If you choose to turn right and explore the village, you may notice a piece of metallic sculpture in the form of a Red Dragon on the front lawn of a certain house.**

6.5 The Red Dragon on the Lawn, Pencarreg

When you pass by this Red Dragon you are passing Gwynfor Evans's house, the present Talar Wen, the same name as the house he and his family lived in for many years near Llangadog. There have been several glimpses already in this guide into the life and work of this remarkable human being, Gwynfor Evans. At this point, at the foothills of the Pencarreg peak with its television transmitter, it is appropriate to describe Gwynfor's culminating role in the victory for a Welsh

Gwynfor's Red Dragon

television station, when in May 1980 he made a dramatic announcement. The story has not been told better than by Dafydd Williams in his *The Story of Plaid Cymru*:

Calling on the government to honour its promise to Wales, he stated his intention to begin a hunger strike in the autumn, a 'fast unto death' as the newpapers put it.

No-one doubted his resolve. Many nationalists were horrified at the prospect. Before the public announcement two party officials travelled to his Llangadog home. They hoped to persuade him not to go ahead – but Gwynfor Evans was adamant: his concern was to hammer out precise details of the campaign.

Once the die was cast, Plaid Cymru members rallied round their leader. A series of major rallies began in the summer with the object of demonstrating mass support. It rapidly became apparent that Gwynfor Evans had accurately gauged the strength of public opinion. Twenty-two meetings had been arranged for the Plaid leader in Wales between 6 September and the date set for beginning his hunger strike in Llangadog, Sunday 5 October. Two thousand people packed Cardiff's Sophia Gardens Pavilion at the beginning of the campaign, and all the rallies proved successful. By giving the government five months warning, the Plaid president had ensured they were subject to maximum pressure. The Archbishop of Wales, the Right Reverend Gwilym O.Williams, Sir Cennydd Treharne, Sir Goronwy Daniel, Lord Cledwyn and Michael Foot were among prominent figures who intervened.

Finally on 17 September, almost exactly a year after Mr Whitelaw's speech, the government caved in. Talks between the new Welsh Secretary Nicholas Edwards and representatives of 'moderate opinion' provided the cover used to beat a hasty retreat. The Welsh television channel would go ahead after all. A well-timed slogan ingeniously painted on the river wall of the House of Commons summed it up: 'GWYNFOR 1 – THATCHER 0'. It was the government's first U-turn.

Sianel Pedwar Cymru finally took to the air in 1982. It was rapidly to win its place in the life of Wales, broadcasting 25 hours a week in Welsh at peak viewing hours. Once its course was set, the government stuck to its commitments on finance, and Welsh broadcasters found there was no shortage of talent for the new service. A whole new industry of independent Welsh television producers sprang up. By 1990, when Gwynfor Evans opened a £5 million studio for the Barcud company of Caernarfon, S4C and its ancillaries employed as many people as did deep coal-mines in Wales.

The battle for Welsh television provided the national movement with a welcome victory at a bleak time in its history. For the many friends and followers of Gwynfor Evans the outcome was also an enormous relief.

V. We drive now to the scene of Gwynfor Evans's electoral victory in Carmarthen (Caerfyrddin) in 1966, a milestone in Welsh political history. We can on the way make one brief detour to see another milestone.

Proceed south on A485 through Llanybydder for several miles; after the village of New Inn, look out for an unnumbered road to the right signposted to Pencader. It is about a mile to the village and the 'milestone' we are seeking. At the main road, turn right, and look for a low wall on the left, with a slate tablet placed rather inconspicuously in it.

6.6 Plaque for the Old Man of Pencader

It is here that 'some old man of these people', as Giraldus Cambrensis tells it at the close of his *Description of Wales*, was questioned by Henry II during the king's progress through Wales of 1163. As to Wales's future as a nation, the old man of Pencader is quoted as saying the following:

> 'This nation, O King, may now, as in future times, be harassed, and in a great measure weakened and destroyed by your and other powers; but it can never be totally subdued through the wrath of man, unless the wrath of God shall concur. Nor do I think that any other nation than this of Wales, or any other language, whatever may hereafter come to pass, shall on the day of severe examination before the Supreme Judge, answer for this corner of the earth.'

This is the reply memorialized by the plaque.

VI.   From Pencader take the road south (B4459) to rejoin A485, which in turn joins A40 just before Carmarthen is reached. Guild Hall Square is best come upon by keeping to the south side of the city along the river, then turning up where you see signs to the bus station. Parking is possible in Guild Hall Square.

6.7 The Guildhall Balcony, Carmarthen (14 July 1966)

Gwynfor Evans had been a member of the Carmarthenshire County Council since 1949 – sixteen years. That counted for a lot. It was a by-election and no majority in the House of Commons was at stake, which set aside the old slogan about 'wasting your vote'. Gwynfor made the future of Wales the election issue, and won. Phil Williams has written of this time in his autobiographical *Voice From the Valleys* (1981):

> It was one of the most enjoyable fortnights of my life and from the beginning there was the scent of victory in the summer air. I am enough of a determinist to know that the breakthrough was

coming . . . I remember Chris Rees bringing an enthusiastic report from Scotland of how the tide was turning. But how appropriate that the first honour should go to Gwynfor.

A week after election night and Gwynfor's standing on the balcony which you can see on the front of the Guildhall, a good many of the people who had been in the crowd formed a large caravan of automobiles and buses, and set off across the Black Mountains to help cheer Gwynfor into his seat in Westminster. There was an immediate clash with the system when he was prevented by the Speaker from taking the oath in Welsh. And so it went . . .

Gwynfor was elected in subsequent elections, and there are now several Plaid Cymru MPs sitting in Westminster. But 1966 was the breakthrough, when emotions ran high. Harri Webb, the Anglo-Welsh poet, wrote 'A ballad of the fourteenth of July', which reads in part:

> In the square before the Guildhall
> We gathered two thousand strong,
> And as far as Abergwili
> They could hear the triumphal song.
>
> When Gwynfor got in for Carmarthen
> The summer night was sweet,
> The breeze blew in from the hayfields
> And the people danced in the street.

VII. Take the main road east out of Carmarthen (A40 – signposted to Llandeilo); at the major junction, keep on A40, and after a short time, in the village of Abergwili (where, they say, shouting could be heard on election night 1966), look out for the sign to the Carmarthen museum on the right. Turn in to the car park.

6.8 The Bishop's Palace, Abergwili

This is where the bishops of St David's have habitually lived – and sometimes it has actually been a centre of importance, as when Bishop Richard Davies 'kept an exceeding great post', inviting William Salesbury and others there to work on a translation into Welsh of the New Testament, the Psalms, and

The Bishop's Palace

the Book of Common Prayer. This was 1563-68; so William Morgan had this version to work from in doing the whole Bible later. Davies was 'a good bishop of St David's', says *The Oxford Companion to the Literature of Wales*, 'battling against spiritual indifference and defending his diocese against greedy laymen.' Some of the relics of this battle are on show in the Palace, now Carmarthen County Museum, open Monday to Saturday, free admission. It is worth a visit; Gwynfor Evans has called Abergwili the 'headquarters of the Renaissance in Wales.'

VIII. Continue on A40 east along the river Tywi, and turn right to cross it on B4297. There is a pleasant little picnic site by the river on the right-hand side of the road; park and walk over to the castle on the opposite side of the road.

6.9 Lord Rhys's Dryslwyn Castle

These Welsh princes were no fools: they chose the loveliest places to live in. Lord Rhys built this small castle in about 1160. The fools in this case were the English knights who were standing on it when their own sappers laid charges and blew it up, what a mess, 1287.

At least Dryslwyn Castle is easily accessible. Dinefwr, Lord Rhys's main seat a few miles farther up river, is out of bounds to the public because of unsafe conditions – the most you will get is a glimpse of it across the river as you approach Llandeilo. Its neglect has been pointed out continually by Gwynfor Evans as a national shame. Cadw, a government agency, are now working on it.

We now take the road that Gwynfor used to drive along to Carmarthen for County Council meetings: 'twenty-five years – a million miles!'

IX. Cross the river bridge and turn left on B4300 east towards Llandeilo. Before reaching the town, the road joins A476, and then A483 north. Park on the sloping street by the cemetery, on the left as you enter Llandeilo. Just round the corner on the busy main street is the unique Cawdor Hotel for an interesting REST STOP – one of a kind, nothing else like it in Wales.

Leave Llandeilo on A40; about 2 miles out of town, look for an unmarked turn on the left, just after the sign announcing Manordeilo. Take the unnumbered road up to Cwmifor village, and stop at the Baptist chapel.

6.10 Cwmifor Chapel and the Rebecca Protests

We visit this particular chapel because we know that in August 1843 there were Rebecca meetings here, and a London *Times* correspondent was allowed to attend one of them. He received the assistance of an interpreter, explains David Williams in his book on the *Rebecca Riots*. The Resolutions were dated 'the first year of Rebecca's exploits, AD 1843', and the Preamble was that the price of liberty is eternal vigilance. 'An army of principles,' said Rebecca, 'will penetrate where an army of soldiers cannot.' The grievances included the high cost of

Cwmifor Chapel

tolls, tithes and church rents. There was also a resolution that 'no Englishman shall be employed as a steward in Wales.' Small tenant farmers were the people in attendance, and were all 'Rebecca'.

We can now find an actual preserved toll-house not far away.

Continue on this side road, bearing right at the first junction, keeping right at the next junction, and ignoring the right turn at the next junction, and going on till the road itself turns right. At that turn, on the left, is one of the toll-houses that the Rebecca movement was about. The hexagonal structure would originally have been thatched.

Old toll-house

Proceeding down the road for about ½ mile, you come to the main road A40; opposite is the road over the bridge into Llangadog (A4069). Cross the Tywi, and go through the town that was Gwynfor Evans's home locality for many years.

X. Continue out of town on A4069 to Llandovery, and join A40 east for about 2 miles until you see a signpost to Pentre-tŷ-gwyn and Babel; take this left turn, and follow the signs to Pantycelyn. You know you have arrived when you see a new sign in blue inviting you into 'Cartref William Williams Pantycelyn.'

130

6.11 Pantycelyn

At Pantycelyn you are at one of the great centres of Welsh
identity. Farmhouses in Wales contain history, and this one
especially does. It is a working uplands farm, but the family,
descendants of William Williams Pantycelyn, also want to
make it available to you as a shrine, so that you can know the
source of that great hymn 'Guide me, O Thou Great Jehovah'.

Saunders Lewis called William Williams Pantycelyn 'the
great discoverer of the unconscious, the strong-hold of the
passions . . . the first poet of science and the modern mind.'
And I thought Pantycelyn was only a hymn-writer! But listen
to this stanza:

> Search, my soul, to your heart's corners,
>> Search the long paths thoroughly,
> And search all the secret chambers
>> That within its limits be.

If he is serious – as he must be – this is dangerous stuff. These
great revival meetings of the triumvirate, Daniel Rowland,
Howell Harris and Williams Pantycelyn, must have tapped
deep imaginal, aesthetic and archetypal rivers of emotion. A
great deal has to do with the Welsh language itself, the
affective history of individual words and complexes of social
and religious and sexual longing involved in metaphoric
language. Gwynfor Evans in *Land of My Fathers* cites the
following hymn of Pantycelyn's as an example of the
'extremely fine lyrical poems which have become a priceless
part of the personality of every cultured Welshman':

> 'Rwy'n edrych dros y bryniau pell
>> Amdanat bob yr awr;
> Tyrd, fy anwylyd, mae'n hwyrhau,
>> A'm haul bron mynd i lawr.
>
> Melysach nag yw'r diliau mêl
>> Yw munud o'th fwynhau,
> Ac nid oes gennyf bleser sydd
>> Ond hynny yn parhau.
>
> A phan y syrthio sêr y nen
>> Fel ffigys ir i'r llawr,
> Bydd fy niddanwch heb ddim trai
>> Oll yn fy Arglwydd mawr.
>
> I look across the distant hills
>> each hour for thy coming:

come, my loved one, for it's late
and my sun's near to setting.

Sweeter than the honey drops
a minute's joy in thee,
and I've no other pleasure that
lasts everlastingly.

And when the stars of heaven fall
like ripe figs to the sward,
there'll be no ebb to the delight
that's all in my great Lord.

Williams Pantycelyn was the chief organiser of the Methodist fellowship meeting, where problems were discussed and his wisdom sought. By the year 1750 there were about 430 of them in Wales, the basis for Methodist strength. The travel involved was prodigious. He calculated in his old age that he had travelled 148,000 miles, spending almost as much time on horseback as at home. 'It was on horseback,' says Gwynfor Evans in his *Welsh Nation Builders*, 'that he did much of his reading and composed many of his hymns.' This sounds very much like Gwynfor himself; no wonder the fellow-feeling.

At Pantycelyn you can see the clock that comes down from the time of the poet. For a more imposing monument, we must go to his burial place back in the town.

> *Retrace your steps to A40, turning right and proceeding into the centre of Llandovery, where you take A483 (towards Llanwrtyd Wells) for a short distance. Look out for the Hospital; the turn off you are seeking is the first to the left after the hospital buildings. Drive up the lane of trees, and you will see the church gates, where you may park.*

6.12 Monument of William Williams Pantycelyn

This church of Llanfair-ar-y-bryn Parish has a great many interesting features. It stands on the site of a Roman Fort, and began as a monastic cell, which was rebuilt in the 13th century. More alterations were made at the end of the 15th century, and more in 1880, every two or three hundred years, it seems.

We come here to see the last resting place of William Williams Pantycelyn, which, because of the time of his death, 1791, will perforce have had to be in consecrated ground of the established church, even though his preaching had been mainly in unconsecrated open spaces. The epitaph reads:

> He laboured in the service of the Gospel for near half a century and continued incessantly to promote it both by his Labours and Writings; and to his inexpressible Joy beheld its influence extending and its efficacy witnessed in the Conviction and conversion of many thousands.

The famous portrait of Williams Pantycelyn, found still on many mantlepieces, is that of a fresh young man, almost like a new film star.

XI. From the church, return to the main road A483, turn right, the way you came, but immediately look for an unnumbered road on the right signposted to Cil-y-cwm and Rhandir-mwyn. This road follows Afon Tywi up towards the mountains. At a fork, take the road signposted to Rhandir-mwyn. When you gain that village, after several miles there is a suitable REST STOP at the 'Royal Oak Inn'.

As you proceed north you pass the location of Twm Siôn Cati's cave, the hide-out of the Welsh Robin Hood, which is, naturally, in a remote inaccessible spot, far too much of a hike. We are making for a place which has more direct connections to the Welsh Nationalist movement and its leader Gwynfor Evans.

Eventually you will see the damsite of Llyn Brianne. Be sure to turn into the first of the viewpoints (unmarked), below the dam, looking up.

6.13 Llyn Brianne Reservoir

The story of this dam is that of an inspired trade-off. The Carmarthen County engineers were all for building a reservoir by damming the Afon Gwendraeth Fach, up above Kidwelly. This would have destroyed a lovely valley, near industrial south Wales, and many farm houses. Gwynfor Evans as County Councillor set to work to find an alternative, and came up with a suitable place where there were no villages, and a dam would not have such bad consequences. Thus, Llyn Brianne is sometimes jocularly called 'Gwynfor's dam'. It turned out to be quite a beautiful compromise: not a single farmhouse was drowned.

Llyn Brianne

XII. The proposed route back to Aberystwyth around Llyn Brianne is winding and strenuous, but can be enjoyable, if taken slowly.

The road goes around the east side of the reservoir, turning west at the far end of the first of the flanks of water, and turning north at the tip of the second. This new road built for access to the recreational possibilities of the Llyn Brianne area, finally joins the old drover's road, which linked Llanwrtyd Wells at the east of the mountain range with Tregaron at the west.

(This drover's road was the one used by Gwynfor in walking home to Barry after completing his first year at the University College, Aberystwyth.)

6.14 Statue of Henry Richard (1812-1888), Tregaron

Do not leave Tregaron without paying respects to Henry Richard, whose full-length statue in Tregaron town square can hardly be avoided. Here is a congenial figure with which to end our day in 'Gwynfor's Country'. One can tell he had a benign personality and a wide sensibilty. A native of Tregaron, Richard is buried in London; he lived and worked there, but he never turned his back on his homeland. When he entered Parliament as MP for Merthyr Tydfil at the age of fifty-six he was hailed as the 'Member for Wales' – 'the first real exponent in the House of Commons of the Puritan and progressive life in Wales,' Tom Ellis said of him. In a speech to the voters of Merthyr, Henry Richard is quoted by his biographer Charles S.Miall as follows:

Henry Richard

> You knew me. You knew that though my lot was cast in London, yet I had been loyal in heart to the old land of my birth, the scene of my childhood's joys, and the place of my fathers' sepulchres; you knew that I had never missed an opportunity to do what I could to promote the religious, educational, and political interests of my country; and you knew that I had done all in my power to repel the base and groundless calumnies by which our natural reputation had been defamed.

In this last comment, Richard is referring to his prominent speeches repudiating the infamous Blue Books on Welsh education (see Introduction, above). He had the courage of his convictions. His first act in Parliament was to move a resolution condemning the conduct of landlords in evicting their Welsh tenants who had voted liberal in the election. Facing him, says his biographer, 'was a phalanx of the very men whose offence he was about to expose. But with full command over himself and his materials, and sustained by his moral courage and high patriotic purpose, he spoke for about an hour with perfect self-possession and fervid eloquence.' He was a pacifist when it was unpopular, and a key supporter of the idea of a League of Nations when it was being scoffed at. I see these qualities in the statue in the square. D.Samuel, writing in the *Transactions of the Cardiganshire Antiquarian Society*, has put it decorously:

> The pose represents its subject, as should always be the case with statues of statesmen and orators, in standing attitude. It portrays Mr Richard holding his eye-glasses in one hand, and leaning slightly forward, as if the orator had just removed them from his eyes and was bent on pressing home some particular point in his oration. The right hand grasps a folio of notes, upon which the word 'Peace' stands forth conspicuous.

The boyhood home of Henry Richard, which has a plaque, can be seen by walking across the Teifi bridge and to the rear of the pub next to the National Westminster Bank building.

XIII. Take A485 west out of Tregaron, which joins A487 into Aberystwyth.

Day 7

Saints and Sinners

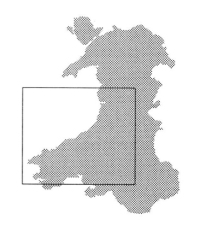

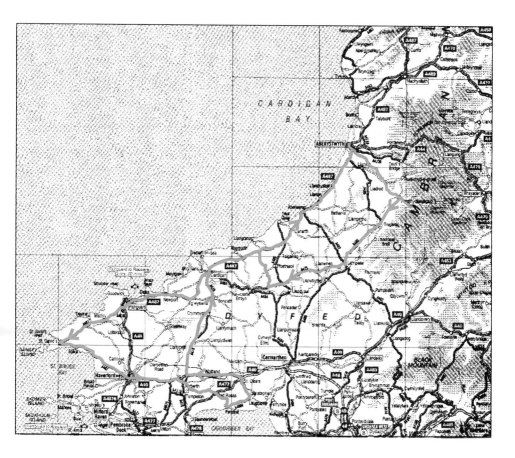

DAY 7: Saints and Sinners

Caradoc Evans and Dylan Thomas do not fit everybody's idea of a proper Cymro. We shall call them 'sinners' – though Dafydd ap Gwilym may have been of the same breed. The patron saint is St David, but 'saint' may be applied without irony to others.

I	Take A487 south out of Aberystwyth, then B4340 to New Cross – and Capel Horeb (7.1)
II	Continue on B4340 to Ystrad Meurig and the School (7.2)
III	Continue on B4340 to B4343 and turn right into Pontrhydfendigaid – take the unnumbered road left to Strata Florida (7.3)
IV	Return to B4343, and proceed south through Tregaron to Llanddewibrefi and St David's church (7.4)
V	Proceed on B4343, turn right on A482 through Llanbedr Pont Steffan, and left on A475; turn right on B4334 to Hawen and Rhydlewis (7.5)
VI	Continue north on B4334, turn left on A487 through Aberteifi (Cardigan), and turn right on B4582 to Nevern church (7.6)
VII	Proceed south on B4582 to meet A487 again, turn right, passing Fishguard (Abergwaun) to St David's (Tyddewi) and the cathedral (7.7)
VIII	Leave St David's on A487 east through Haverfordwest to A40 and the turn-off on to B4314 to Narberth (7.8)

138

IX   Continue on B4314 east to Pendine and A4066 to
        Laugharne (7.9)

X   Take A4066 north out of Laugharne, turn right on
        A40 west to Whitland and the Hywel Dda Memorial
        Square (7.10)

XI   Continue west on A40, turn right on to A478 north,
        passing Efail-wen, and taking the unnumbered
        road left to Mynachlog-ddu (7.11) and the Presely
        Hills (7.12)

XII   Regain A478, and proceed north, joining A487 to
        enter Cardigan (7.13)

XIII   Continue north on A487, turn left on A486 to New
        Quay (7.14)

XIX   Return via B4342 to A487, and proceed north
        stopping at St David's church (7.15) before
        proceeding on A487 back to Aberystwyth.

I. Take A487 south to Southgate; then take B4340 (the odd fifth road of the the crossroads, signposted to Trawsgoed) about 3 miles to New Cross. Park at Capel Horeb on the right-hand side of the road; climb the path behind the chapel to Caradoc Evans's gravestone at the top of the field. The flat gravestone is at the back row where the five stone steps lead up.

7.1 Grave of Caradoc Evans (1878-1945), New Cross

In one of her biographical books on her husband, Marguerite Evans writes:

> A farmer whose fields were not far from our house used gin-traps, and night after night we would be awakened by the screaming of the little animals caught in those cruel iron jaws.
>
> Caradoc tackled the farmer, who told him to mind his own business. That determined Caradoc, so when it was late enough and he was quite sure there was no one about he would tour the field 'confiscating' as many traps as he could find.
>
> When he brought them back in a sack I said: 'That's stealing, Caradoc. We'll have a policeman calling to ask questions next.'
>
> 'Let him, and I'll tell him, and let's hope it gets in all the newspapers. Dickens did away with debtors' prisons. Down with gin-traps, me!'

This seems to me the essential Caradoc Evans. He cannot stand the pain that is done to dumb creatures (and that includes human victims) by the cold avaricious self-righteous petty powerful. All his stories can be considered confiscating gin-traps.

We shall visit the place that gave Caradoc his beginnings (7.5); here he spent the last fourteen years of his life, up to the time when sickness took him into Aberystwyth. His wife has described him 'in the midst of his people. . . Here the true Caradoc emerged, the man who, though he condemned the weaknesses and follies in all human nature, using the Welsh in particular only because he knew them so well, yet loved his country with a fervour which made him a true son of Wales.' George H.Green, writing a memoir for Caradoc's posthumous collection of stories *The Earth Gives All and Takes All* (1946) said:

> It was quite in keeping with the strong feeling he evoked in Wales
> that, on the very day on which an anonymous journalist wrote of
> him as 'the most hated man in Wales,' six Cardiganshire farmers
> bore him on their shoulders to the summit of the hill where his
> grave had been dug, and the minister of a Welsh 'chapel'
> committed his remains to the earth. From that day on, someone in
> the village has strewn fresh flowers daily on his grave.

Horeb chapel

Mrs Towers of Llandre once told me who she thought had tended the grave. For a number of years she was in service in New Cross and walked by Caradoc's house each Sunday to the chapel. Often he would be sitting at the open window, and would joke with them about the length of the sermon. In Mrs Towers's words: 'He was all right, Caradoc.'

I believe that Caradoc Evans will eventually be acknowledged as *the* world-class writer of the twentieth-century Anglo-Welsh. This is far too large a statement to try to justify, but as you read the inscription that he wrote for his own gravestone you will get some sense of the power and rightness of his prose:

> 'Bury me lightly so that the small rain
> may reach my face and the fluttering
> of the butterfly shall not escape my ear.'

Not only the words but the burial spot was his choice: you will see, as he wanted to see forever, a view from this rise of hill in West Wales unequalled anywhere.

Caradoc's house 'Bryn Awelon' is the first gate on the right past the chapel as you proceed south on B4340.

II. After about 7 miles on B4340 you will drive through the village of Ystrad Meurig, and you will see the old school building to the left of the road. Across the road, behind houses, is the grassy mound referred to in the quotation below.

7.2 Ystrad Meurig School of Edward Richard (1714-1777)

> He would rise early with the dawn and stroll to the tumulus on which the old Welsh castle of Ystrad Meurig once stood, and with the glorious vistas of 'Cors Goch Caron' [now a Nature Reserve] in front of him would gladly surrender to the demanding charms of the Muse, who despite her Greek origin, spoke to Edward Richard in the incomparable cadences of the Welsh language.

Thus wrote the last headmaster of the school about the original founder of St John's College. It is very much to the point that the Muse also spoke to Edward Richard in Greek and Latin. For it was mainly to learn those languages that he gave up his post at the village school and secluded himself for six years. He could not afford to go to a centre of scholarship, but worked from 4 am every day alone in the village church on Classics, Mathematics, and Divinity, in a courageous act of foresight and determination, so that when he started up the pioneering secondary school he wanted, the pupils would be able to get from him the syllabus that could take them to Oxford or Cambridge.

After a long and successful teaching life here at St John's College, as he called his school, he included in his will an endowment that he felt sure would mean its continuation in perpetuity. 'Let the school and library be kept in good repair and improved,' he wrote. And so it was for two hundred years.

III. Continue on B4340 to the junction with B4343, and bear right into the village of Pontrhydfendigaid ('Bridge of the ford of the Blessed'). After the hump bridge, look for the sign on the left to Strata Florida, and drive the unnumbered road for about

7.3 Strata Florida Abbey and the Grave of Dafydd ap Gwilym

Founded in the 12th century, this Abbey (Ystrad Fflur, in Welsh – 'Plain of Flower') was for many decades the political and educational as well as the religious centre of Wales. Many important Welsh manuscripts were copied here. The sheep-rearing lands owned by the monastery provided immense wealth and prestige. Llywelyn the Great chose this place in which to call all the Welsh princes together in 1238 for the ritual swearing of allegiance to his son.

In spite of the fact that Dafydd ap Gwilym prophesied that he would be buried in a grove of birches, tradition has him under the yew tree here at Ystrad Fflur, a belief that may have been derived from an erroneous reading of Gruffudd Grug's poem 'The Yew Tree' of late 14th century:

> For the best of lads, yew-tree
> By the wall of Ystrad Fflur,
> May God bless you, bliss of trees,
> Grown as a home for Dafydd.

The latest translator of this poem doesn't think the Dafydd here is Dafydd ap Gwilym, nor can the present yew tree in the church graveyard have been there that long. But the tradition is attractive, and will not go away while native Welsh slate holds the inscription which you may read if you know Latin or Welsh. This is a translation:

> Here under a yew tree, near the wall of Strata Florida, six centuries ago was buried Dafydd ap Gwilym, 'poet whose cywydd was like wine.' Dafydd, thou fair and mighty singer, is it here thou wast laid under green trees? Under a fair bright lusty yew, where thou wast buried, poetry was hidden away.

T.H.Parry-Williams (5.15) spoke at the dedication of the plaque.

IV. *Return to the highway (B4343), turn left, and proceed south through Tregaron. Stay on B4343 for about three miles down to Llanddewibrefi, where you will have no difficulty finding St David's church, with parking at the churchyard gate.*

7.4 The Holy Ground of Llanddewibrefi

As every Welsh schoolchild knows, St David was the son of Sant, the King of Ceredigion, great-grandson of Cunedda's son Ceredig. His mother's name was Non. He was educated near Aberaeron on the coast, and ultimately founded a monastic community where the famous St David's Cathedral now stands (see below 7.7). David achieved first place among his peers, and he did so here at Llanddewibrefi. A large gathering of clerics had met to discuss and condemn the Pelagian heresy. Apparently the arguments were faltering, and some intervention was crucial. Paulinus, David's teacher, called him forward. As he addressed the huge assembly the ground rose miraculously under his feet, and he spoke as though from a raised platform and his voice sounded like a trumpet. Because of this miracle the heresy was successfully extirpated. The present church stands on the hillock that resulted from Dewi Sant being given his special pulpit and his pre-eminence by acclamation – not by fiat from Rome, one may add. In this, Dewi Sant is a symbol of Welsh independence, as he was in his ecclesiastical policies.

V. *Proceed south on B4343; at the junction with A482, turn right, through the town centre of Llanbedr Pont Steffan, and take the left road at the junction A475 south (towards Newcastle Emlyn). After about 16 miles, after crossing A486 look out for B4334. Turn right, and soon after crossing the intersection with B4571 the road takes you downhill into the village of Hawen, dominated by a large chapel on the right. If it is not open, the key may be obtained from the house opposite.*

7.5 'Capel Sion', Hawen, and Rhydlewis

This chapel is a fine example of nonconformist interior style. You will see the rows of seats waiting for the commanding presence at the pulpit, which is so intimately near and yet so dominating. The Bible on the preacher's stand has its spine

'Capel Sion'

broken from much pounding. The ironwork balcony is a distinctive feature of Hawen Chapel.

This is the place where Caradoc Evans went through soul-searing formative experiences in his young life. In later life he wrote about the chapel as he must have felt it then: as a totalitarian system, where absolute power invested in the preacher leads inevitably to authoritarian abuse. As you read the following passage from *Capel Sion,* from the story called 'The Pillars of Sion', you need to know that Caradoc's mother received similar ostracization. She was a widow and lacked the money to pay to the chapel the amount assessed to her. Putting her children first, she refused payment, and was, according to the custom of the day, treated as an outcast. The circumstances in the story are different – here the offence apparently is that a widow brought her schizophrenically disabled daughter to chapel one Sunday in violation of an unwritten rule; but we know from the power of the writing that the feeling comes out of Caradoc's own life.

> Wherefore on the Sabbath she took out her funeral garments and put them on Silah, whom she brought her into Sion; and mother and daughter sat among the hired people in the loft.
>
> The rage of the congregation was high when they comprehended the meaning of this abomination.
>
> 'Ach y fi!' said one. 'A sick old mouse is Becws.'
>
> 'Out of her head is the female,' said another. 'Silah was

conceived in brimstone. The dolt's hair is the colour of flames.'

The praying men said: 'Not right is this, people bach, dear me. Come, now, then, the most religious of us off will go and make phrases to the Respected.'

They went into the House of the Capel, and the chief of them was Amos Penparc, whose riches were above any other man on the floor of Sion, and whose piety was established. Amos stood on the threshold, and the lesser praying men stayed on the flagstone, which is without the door.

'Hello, here!' said Amos. 'Not wishful, religious Respected, are we to disturb his food eating, but there's grave are the words in my head.'

Bern-Davydd answered: 'Come you, boys bach Capel Sion, the son of the Jesus bach will always hearken to you.'

'Well – well, then,' said Amos Penparc. 'What he does not know that Silah the mad bitch sat in Sion this day?'

'Indeed to goodness, Amos bach! Speak you like that, I shouldn't be surprised,' replied Bern-Davydd.

'And did I not observe the female Becws praying her own prayer while he was mouthing to the Great One?' said Amos.

'Don't speak any more, Amos Penparc,' said Bern-Davydd. 'Retch my old food I will. Read you the Speech Book for a small time bach.'

Bern-Davydd finished his eating, and he lifted his voice: 'Don't say!'

'Iss, iss, Respected.'

'Can a carrot turn colour?'

The praying men were amazed.

Amos Penparc said: 'Is not Silah counted an offender in the Palace of White Shirts?'

'Smell is Silah in the Big Man's nose,' said Bern-Davydd.

'Iss, little Respected,' said Amos. 'Fall upon us He will. He will smoulder our little ricks of hay. Speak him then what shall our cattle eat.'

At the close of the day Bern-Davydd, in the presence of all the congregation, addressed the men of the Big Seat: 'Now, then, boys Capel Sion, make proof about Silah the daughter of Becws. Amos Penparc, start, man bach.'

'Well, now, indeed, no,' said Amos. 'Right that the Religious of the Pulpit says sayings.'

'Much liking has the Big Man for you Amos,' said Bern-Davydd.

Amos rose and turned his bland countenance and unclouded eyes upon the assembly, and fastening his coat over his beard, he spoke: 'Important in my pride is Sion. In Sion the Big Man's son dwells.' Then sang Amos Penparc: 'Lord bach, lessen your fury and depart not from us. Has not the Respected made us very religious? Is not the Capel like a well-stocked farm? The seating places are as full as the stables of the *Drovers' Arms* on an old fair day. And there's rising will be from the burial ground when Gabriel bach blows his gold trumpet: there will come up more people than I have sheep on the moor. Good is the Big Male to his photographs.' Amos ceased his song. 'But, people bach, sinful was Becws to bring her mad harlot into Sion. Lots of talk nasty there will be. Can corn grow from the seed of wasteful old thistles? Are mad bitches a glory unto Sion? How says the Respected: "Bad old smell in the Big Man's nose is Silah"? The Temple must be cleansed, indeed, now.'

'Wholesome, male man of Penparc, are your words,' said the Respected Bern-Davydd. 'Close my eyes I will now and say affairs to the Big Man: Jesus bach, wise you are to be with Amos Penparc. Full of wisdom is Amos, and his understanding is higher than the door of Sion, deeper than the whiskers under his waistcoat. Four pillars hold up the loft of Capel Sion, and not one is as strong as Amos. Lias Carpenter can hew the pillars with his saw, but who can hew through Amos? Speak now to us about cleaning the Temple. Mad is Silah, and did not Becws her mother bring her into Sion? Disgrace very bad is this. Lewd was the wench's behaviour, Jesus. Busy am I thinking out sermons, so you come down and tell orderings to Amos Penparc. Amen.'

Bern-Davydd's praise of Amos Penparc was spread abroad, whereof Becws got ashamed of that which she had done.

'Why you are without sense, idiot?' she said to Silah.

Silah did not answer.

'The concubine fach!' said Becws. 'A full barrow of sin is in your inside. Open your neck, you bull calf. Have you not made me wicked in the sight of Sion?'

Lanlas Uchaf

Becws was angry that her daughter was speechless and she did not give her food for two days, and as Silah was yet stubborn she placed her in the pigsty and tied her hands together behind her back so that she could not open the door, and she said to her: 'Stay here, you scarlet crow; eat from the trough and lie with the swine.'

For those who might be interested to see Caradoc Evans's boyhood home, it is still standing, though not easy to find. The road is just past the village post office of Rhydlewis; a right turn, and another right turn, takes you a few hundred yards to Lanlas Uchaf, with a low stone wall and iron gate facing you on your left as you approach. (No plaque.)

VI. Continue from Rhydlewis north on B4334 to A487, turn left and, by-passing Aberteifi (Cardigan), leave A487 where B4582 turns off to the right. At the village of Nanhyfer (Nevern),you will see the old churchyard to the right. Park at the gate.

7.6 The Celtic Crosses of Nevern

Nanhyfer churchyard is a restful spot, which takes one back to

The Great Celtic Cross

remote times; it was founded by St Brynach, a 6th century saint, who is reputed to have been a friend of St David. The present church dates from the 13th century, but the Great Celtic Cross you can see in the churchyard among the cypress trees is older, probably 10th century. It is one of the most perfect specimens of its kind, and you will want to scrutinize all four sides with their different 'ribbon' arrangements symbolising eternity (because, it is said, you cannot find where any of the lines end). Inside the church there are other remarkable stelae, with Gothic runes. (A booklet on the subject is available in the church.) West of the church, over a stile, is a cross cut in the rock; it is called 'the Pilgrim's Cross', because people remember it as an old shrine along the way between the two religious centres, Holywell in the north and St David's, the place we are on our way to.

> **Reach the cross by walking out at the back of the church, keeping left over the stream to join the paved road up to the stile and sign.**

> **VII. Proceed down B4582 the short distance to meet A487 again, turn right and make for Abergwaun (Fishguard). Incidentally, as the road approaches the town on top of a bluff, you can see the 'Lower Town' below at the water's edge: this was the location used for the film version of Under Milk Wood, good location, lamentable film. Take the A40 Haverfordwest road by-pass and look for signs to St David's (A487). Park in the public car park if nothing nearer the cathedral. This is a tourist centre, and you will be offered information at the sign of the 'i'. This is a primary REST STOP.**

7.7 St David's Cathedral

The feast days coming down from very early Irish sources give 1st March as that of St David, as it still is today. One tradition is that he was called 'Aquaticus' ('Water-man' – Dyfrwr in Welsh) because he was a sort of a 'vegan', having a diet of bread, vegetables, and water. What we mainly know of Dewi Sant comes from Rhygyfarch's *Life of David*, written in Latin about 1095, five hundred years after the saint's death, and therefore hagiographic if not mythic. For instance, Rhygyfarch has William the Conqueror himself coming to St David's in 1081 to meet with the powerful Welsh princes of the time,

Gruffydd ap Cynan and Rhys ap Tewdwr. This stooping of the high king to local vassals gives the tone of what St David's has meant in terms of the spirit of Welsh independence.

E.G.Bowen, the historian of St David's, emphasizes the point:

> Rhygyfarch tells us of the visit of the three saints – David, Teilo and Padarn to the Patriarch of Jerusalem to be consecrated to the episcopate. After the completion of due ceremonies, the Patriarch 'supported by Divine choice' promotes 'holy David to the Archiepiscopate'. While it is not necessary to accept the story literally, it is important to note that St David and the two other saints are sent for consecration to the Patriarch of Jerusalem and not to the Pope in Rome. From this it is easy to appreciate that Celtic Christians, like Rhygyfarch, were not only prepared to look to the Eastern Church for authority in ecclesiastical matters, but also (as Rhygyfarch certainly does) to use this and other stories to strengthen their political argument for the independence of St David's and its Celtic ecclesiastical background from Canterbury and Rome.
>
> We should not forget that Celtic Christianity and the awareness of its separateness from Rome survived long at St David's. In the Middle Ages Giraldus Cambrensis did all he could to revive it, and travelled to Rome to argue the independence of St David's from the See of Rome, face to face with Pope Innocent III (possibly the greatest Pope ever to sit on the throne of St Peter). Innocent could not agree, and indicated (as one would expect) that he was unable to find in the Papal archives anything that indicated that St David was ever made the Archbishop of a separate province. Independence, however, came with the Disestablishment of the Church in Wales in 1920, and, significantly, it was followed by a memorable event in St David's Cathedral when the first Archbishop of Wales and his Brother Bishops entertained the Eastern Patriarchs of Jerusalem, Alexandria and Byzantium, as symbol of the time-honoured links between East and West in the story of the Christian Church.

The Giraldus Cambrensis mentioned in this quotation, the 'Gerald of Wales' of the famous Latin *Description of Wales* (1193), is reputed to be buried in the Cathedral, with an effigy in the South Choir Aisle next to that of his kinsman and hero The Lord Rhys (1132-1197), the greatest of the South Wales princes. King Henry II's state visit to St David's in 1171 acknowledged Lord Rhys's claims over the whole of Deheubarth. Lord Rhys had a row with Rome, and died excommunicate over the question of Welsh ecclesiastical independence.

VIII. From St David's continue on A487 going east through Haverfordwest (Welsh name, Hwlffordd), where you pick up A40 east, until the right turn on to B4314 to Narberth (Welsh, Arberth). At the south end of the village are the remains of a castle, associated with the story of Pwyll. As you drive by (there is no suitable place to stop), you may imagine its ancient history.

7.8 Pwyll of Arberth

'Pwyll, Prince of Dyfed, was lord of the seven cantrefs of Dyfed, and once upon a time he was at Arberth, his chief palace, and he was minded to go hunt . . .': thus begins the first 'branch' of the *Mabinogi*. Pwyll walks up to the top of a mound that was above the palace, and called Gorsedd Arberth: 'whoever sits upon it cannot go thence without either receiving blows or else seeing a wonder.' The 'wonder' that Pwyll saw was the beautiful Rhiannon riding by, and when he tried on his best horse to overtake her she magically stayed ahead of him until she was ready to speak to him. Since no one has any idea which hillock is the faery Gorsedd Arberth, the serious researcher will presumably have to try several until the wonder comes, or the blows.

IX. Remain on B4314 east out of Narberth (signposted to Princes Gate, and Tavernspite); after the descent into Pendine take A4066 into Laugharne.

7.9 Dylan Thomas's Laugharne

This proposed way of entering Laugharne (pronounce 'Larne'; the Welsh name is Talacharn) is for a reason. The view you get as you drive down from the high point, just before Laugharne, is probably what Dylan Thomas is writing about in his well-known 'Poem in October'. He describes himself walking out of Laugharne up a 'high hill' early on a birthday morning, and looking back on the town:

> Pale rain over the dwindling harbour
> And over the sea wet church the size of a snail
> With its horns through mist and the castle
>
> Brown as owls . . .

But also, from this vantage, the poet could look across the estuary of the River Taf to what were literally the scenes of his childhood, Fern Hill farm and Llan-gain where he often stayed with relatives; in

Laugharne Castle

other words, he is looking back on his past,

> . . .when he walked with his mother
> Through the parables
> Of sun light
> And the legends of the green chapel . . .

He is reflecting on his innocent years, 'where a boy / In the listening / Summertime of the dead whispered the truth of his joy.' This route into Laugharne gives one a chance to see the countryside of the early Dylan in the distance, before coming down to the later Dylan and Browns Hotel.

George Tremlett

In the village, park in the public car park by the water with a good view of Laugharne Castle, remains of. Walk up the main street to Browns Hotel and liquid REST STOP; visit the bookshop opposite and talk to George Tremlett, who has written books on Thomas. The road east of the

> *town is now signposted 'Dylan's Walk'; you will come first to*
> *the little shed on the top path, where the poems were written,*
> *then to the Boat House itself, open now as a tourist attraction,*
> *where you can see the exhibition, get the feel of the place, and*
> *have a sandwich and Welshcake REST STOP.*

This is the place to read Thomas's 'Over Sir John's Hill' –
for the hill itself is seen opposite, across the bay; and you
might light upon

> . . . the fishing holy stalking heron
> In the river Towy below . . .

It is also a good place to read *Under Milk Wood*, Thomas's play
written for radio; it is largely based on Laugharne and its
characters, though with ingredients from elsewhere (see **7.14**
below). As everyone knows, Dylan roared out his last in
America, but his heart was always here. He may have been a
'sinner' in many ways, but he knew where holy ground was.

> *Proceeding out of Laugharne north on the main street (A4066)*
> *you will come to the parish church on the right. Park and walk*
> *to Thomas's grave, which is marked by a simple white wooden*
> *cross.*

> *X. Continue on A4066 north to join A40 at St Clears by-pass;*
> *go west for about 5 miles to Whitland (Welsh name: Hendy-*
> *gwyn). Turn left at the sign for the Hywel Dda Memorial Square,*
> *just past the large dairy complex.*

7.10 Hywel Dda Memorial, Whitland

Hywel Dda (c. 890-950) is the only Welsh king to have earned
the epithet 'Dda', which means 'the Good'. He was not
bloodthirsty, and loved the rule of law. He unified Wales
peacefully, by inheritance, marriage, and by alliances, and
brought peace by diplomatic relations with Alfred the Great of

Wessex, whose chief counsel was Asser, a former member of the monastic community of St David's. Hywel Dda is most famous for his codified *Laws*, especially the law of *gavelkind*, where the land of the father at death is divided among all the sons, not just the eldest son as in England and elsewhere. This unique form of inheritance worked against the amassing of powerful large units in Wales; in a sense, it was more democratic, but posed problems in rivalries as we have seen with Dafydd 'the Last' (**5.3** above). 'Hywel's law excelled from the point of view of justice,' explains Gwynfor Evans; 'Welsh law was more civilized but it weakened the State. It was when faced with united and imperialistic England on the attack that the Welsh suffered most from the weakness caused by its civilized character.' In *Welsh Nation Builders*, he gives five examples where Welsh law excelled:

The Hywel Dda Memorial

(1) The status of women. There was a long tradition in Wales, found in the Celtic Church as well as in secular life, of giving women an honoured social status. Under *Cyfraith Hywel* women had rights in relation to property which were not given them under English law until 1883. A wife also had a right to compensation if struck by her husband without cause: under English law the wife was the property of her husband, a chattel. If divorced, the Welsh woman received up to half the family property.

(2) Execution. In the 12th century there were proportionately less than a quarter of the number of executions under *Cyfraith Hywel* than occurred under English law seven centuries later.

(3) Methods of proving guilt. Such primitive methods as proving guilt by trial of arms, or through fire or boiling

water, were quite alien to *Cyfraith Hywel*. These were ideas of the dark ages or of closed minds, but they were common in England, as one saw later with the burning of witches, who were commonly old women with confused minds. There was little of this in Wales.

(4) Theft. There was no punishment at all if the purpose of the theft was to stay alive. Compare this with the hanging of children in England for stealing a lamb.

(5) Illegitimate children. In order to explain this point I quote an early statement which compares in humanity with the Scottish Declaration of Arbroath in 1320: 'English law states that no son inherits his patrimony except the father's eldest son by his married wife'; *Cyfraith Hywel* judges that the youngest son has a right to it equal to the eldest, and judges that 'the sin of the father and his wrongdoing should not be set against the son's right to his patrimony'. English law has never attained that standard.

> Professor Dafydd Jenkins, the authority on Cyfraith Hywel, notes the irony that certain aspects of the Welsh law which were superseded by English law in 1536 may now be introduced as enlightened and innovatory reforms over 450 years later.

One notable aspect, now coming into common law as a supposed 20th century innovation, is reparation to the victims of crime.

XI. Continue west on A40, and take a right turn on to A478 north (signposted Cardigan). As you pass through Clunderwen you will notice on the left a street name 'Bro Waldo'. After Efail-wen, where 'Rebecca' destroyed the first toll-gate 13 May 1839, take the unnumbered road left to Mynachlog-ddu, at the five-road junction.

7.11 Waldo Williams (1904-1971), Poet, of Mynachlog-ddu

Waldo Williams was a saintly man, who had a vision of the kinship of all persons in the world, and lived by this law of brotherhood, breaking some of the laws which would force him to contribute to war and other acts of inhumanity. He was imprisoned more than once because of his pacifism – even in so-called 'peacetime' in the fifties he refused to pay income tax

155

while conscription into the armed forces existed. Bailiffs came to take away his furniture. 'This was a painful, lonely stance,' write the authors of *Profiles*:

> To most people he was merely an eccentric: no-one else bothered about conscription, but he nagged and nagged against the authorities. Eventually he gave up his post as a teacher, when income tax began to be deducted at source, and became an university extra-mural lecturer, because in that post it was his own responsibility to pay income tax. It is difficult for us to realize the strength of his feeling on this matter: his sense of guilt at man's inhumanity to man was felt almost as a physical pain.

His child-like political honesty meant that he could not bear to go out in the street to face other people at one period during the Korean War. The decline of the Welsh language in Mynachlog-ddu, and rural Wales generally, was to him like 'the loss of the five senses'. It drove this shy man to stand as a Plaid Cymru parliamentary candidate as an extension of his poetry.

Gwyn Jones included Waldo Williams's poem 'In Two Fields' in the *Oxford Book of Welsh Verse in English* (1977) in his own translation. It was in the gap between two fields named in the poem that Waldo, as he described it, 'suddenly and vividly realized, in a very definite personal experience, that people are above all else brothers to one another':

> He stirred my soul where nothing stirred
> Save the sun's thought spinning the haze into verse,
> The ripe gorse clicking in the hedgerows,
> The host of rushes dreaming the blue sky.
> Who is it calls when the imagination wakens
> 'Rise, walk, dance, look on creation!'?
> Who is it hides in the midst of the words?
> – These things on Weun Parc y Blawd and Parc y Blawd.

You will not be able to find the two fields of this poem very easily, but there is a memorial plaque to Waldo Williams outside the village. It names three of the mountain peaks around Mynachlog-ddu, Foel Drygarn, Carn Gyfrwy, and Tal Mynydd, and quotes some of Waldo's lines:

> *Mur fy mebyd*
> (Wall of my youth)
> *Wrth fy nghefn*
> (at my back)

Ym mhob annibyniaeth barn.
(in all independence of thought.)

To find the memorial stones, turn left at the junction in the village and then right, up a road signposted Rosebush. A few hundred yards past the cattle grid, on the left-hand side of the road, at some distance off the road is a naturally placed monolith, with flat ground for parking.

Retrace your steps to the village junction and proceed north-east on the unnumbered road out of Mynachlog-ddu. The peaks named on the Waldo Williams plaque can be seen to the west and ahead. At Carn-meini, less than a mile from the village, you are very close to the place from which the 'blue stones' of Stonehenge were quarried.

7.12 Presely Hills, Origin of Stonehenge

Stones up to four tons were dragged from Mynydd Presely south to the seacoast and shipped some 140 miles to the site of the famous Stonehenge in Wiltshire: no mean feat of communal effort for around 2000 BC. It is not only Waldo Williams who felt the magical properties of these mountains; from time immemorial they have held ritual power. The *Mabinogi* story 'Culhwch and Olwen' has King Arthur confronting the mythic wild boar Twrch Trwyth at the highest point of the Presely range (1760 ft) due west of Mynachlog-ddu. Two of Arthur's sons were killed in this encounter, and have memorial stones there.

XII. Make for Crymych and A478 again; turn left and proceed north for several miles, joining A487 just before entering Cardigan (Aberteifi). There is no need to stop at the castle you see from the road, but one might remember a significant event associated with it.

7.13 Aberteifi and the Cardigan Eisteddfod

This is the traveller Thomas Pennant's account of the first ever eisteddfod, as he heard of it:

> In 1176, the lord Rhys, prince of South Wales, made a great feast at Christmas, on account of the finishing of his new castle at Aberteifi, of which he proclaimed notice through all Britain a year and a day before; great was the resort of strangers, who were nobly entertained, so that none departed unsatisfied. Among deeds of arms, and variety of spectacles, Rhys invited all the bards of Wales, and provided chairs for them, which were placed in his hall, where they sat and disputed and sang, to shew their skill in their respective faculties: after which he bestowed great rewards and rich gifts on the victors. The bards of North Wales won the prizes; but the minstrels of Rhys's household excelled in their faculty. On this occasion the Brawdwr Llys, or judge of the court, an officer fifth in rank, declared aloud the victor, and received from the bard, for his fee, a mighty drinking-horn, made of the horn of an ox, a golden ring, and the cushion on which he sat in his chair of dignity.

The Cardigan National Eisteddfod of 1976 celebrated the eight hundredth anniversary of this event.

XIII. Continue from Aberteifi north on A487; at the crossroads of Post Mawr (Synod Inn), turn left on to A486 to New Quay. Take Church St straight ahead and park near the Pier if you can, for seafront REST STOP.

7.14 New Quay, under 'Milk Wood'

The Black Lion public house on the front has a 'commemorative' mural celebrating the general assumption that it was the model for the 'Sailors' Arms' pub in Dylan Thomas's *Under Milk Wood*. The poet wrote a first draft of this play as a radio talk 'Quite Early One Morning', broadcast in December 1944 while he was resident with his family in New Quay, as far away from the war as he could get. New Quay corresponds as much to the physical setting of *Under Milk Wood* as does Laugharne. Having driven from the top of the town to the bottom you will get a sense of the letters passing between Mog Edwards and Myfanwy Price, and you may see someone like Nogood Boyo idling in a dory in the harbour.

The shack the Thomas family lived in was 'Majoda', now much remodelled, near the sea cliffs along the road we take east out of New Quay.

> **XIX. Take the alternative route (B4342) back to A487; turn left and proceed north towards Aberaeron. Before reaching that port, look out for St David's Church on the left just past Ffos-y-ffin village.**

7.15 Hen Fynyw, St David's School

Rhygyfarch's *Life of St David* says that this was the patron saint's homeland. His father, Sant, ruled Ceredigion from here, Hen Fynyw, where Dewi was first educated under Bishop Guistilianus before going for further instruction to St Paulinus in northern Carmarthenshire. 'It is worth noting,' writes E.G.Bowen,

> that the site of the monastery at Hen Fynyw is typical of so many such monasteries, around the coasts of Wales in the time of David. We note the narrow steep-sided valley running down off the coastal plateau with the monastic site in the upper reaches of the valley, where the land opens out, set in an excellent position by way of the narrow valley cleft to maintain direct communication with the coast. The sea, we recall, was the chief means of movement and the highway of traffic for people and goods at this time.

You might well feel that the sea should again become the principal means of transportation between Wales's seacoast towns as you join the (no doubt) crowded summer traffic on A487 back to Aberystwyth.

Day 8

Hwyl and Farewell

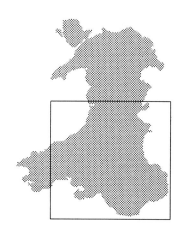

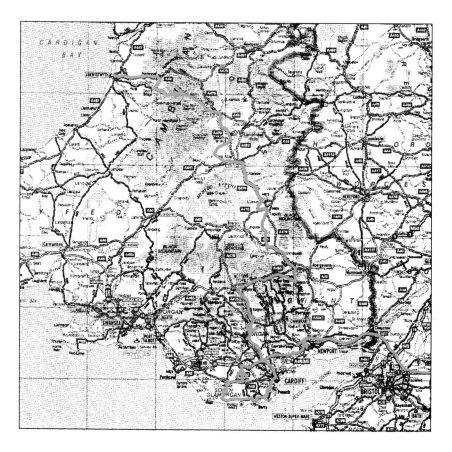

DAY 8: Hwyl and Farewell

We leave Wales, taking a rather arduous journey through South Wales before crossing the Severn Bridge.

I	**Take A44 east from Aberystwyth, turn right at Ponterwyd on A4120 – to Ysbyty Cynfyn (8.1)**
II	**Proceed down A4120, turn left on B4574; keep left at Cwmystwyth, and take the mountain road to Rhayader. Pick up A470, and turn off on B4358, then left at Llanafan-fawr on the unnumbered road to A483 and the Cilmeri monument (8.2)**
III	**Take A483 east, and pick up A470 in Builth Wells. Take A479 to Talgarth, and turn on B4560 to Coleg Trefeca (8.3)**
IV	**Proceed south on B4560 and east on A40; at Crickhowell turn right across the river on A4077, to Gilwern and Gofilon; take the B4246 road to the 'Big Pit' Blaenavon (8.4)**
V	**Proceed to Bryn-mawr on B4248, then A4047 west – to the Aneurin Bevan monument (8.5)**
VI	**Continue west on A4047, becoming A4048, to A465. Go west to the A470 exit south to Cyfarthfa castle (8.6)**
VII	**Take A470 to Cardiff Centre (8.7)**
VIII	**From the city centre make for Rhoose (Cardiff) Airport and then take B4265 to St Athan; turn right on the unnumbered road to Flemingston (8.8)**

IX	*Go north from Flemingston to A48 and Cowbridge (8.9)*
X	*Take A48 east, then A4232 to M4; thence to the Severn Bridge.*

I. Leave Aberystwyth on A44 east, turning right at Ponterwyd on A4120 towards Devil's Bridge (Pontarfynach). The first stop is about 2 miles down the road at Ysbyty Cynfyn church on the right, rather hidden back off the road.

8.1 The Questionable Stone Circle of Ysbyty Cynfyn Churchyard

Malkin's early travel book of 1804 mentions a single large upright stone monument – the one that is conspicious as you enter the churchyard gate; but in his second edition of 1807 Malkin augments this single monolith into a 'druidical circle':

> I have from numerous appearances in Wales, as well as from a great many passages furnished to me by my literary friends in old Welsh writers, whether historians or poets, been fully persuaded that the first British Christians used the Druidical places of worship in the open air . . . The church and church-yard of Yspytty Kenwyn may be adduced as an instance of this. The church has been built within a large druidical circle or temple. Many of the large stones forming the circle still remain.

What happened to Malkin between the first and second edition? He had not visited this site again; he had, however, visited his relatives in Cowbridge and visited the bookshop of 'Mr Edward Williams, who possesses more real knowledge and conjectural sagacity on antiquarian subjects, than almost any man of his day.' This is, to use the name by which he is best known, Iolo Morganwg, a man of undoubted talents and great wishful thinking. Look for yourself: there is no stone circle here. The stones that form the gateway were presumably put there as part of the churchyard expansion of 1901; but even if you include them, there is still nothing like a circle. There are no stones at the rear of the church. The idea of a circle is a 'psychic fact' deriving from our innate wish to connect the past to the present, so that our world can be vital and interesting rather than dull and empty. We will be tracking Iolo Morganwg down in his Glamorgan territory; and we will find him as Gwynfor Evans has described him 'about the most remarkable genius that Wales ever had' (**8.8**). This guide is written in the belief that Wales is interesting enough without the heightened 'conjectural sagacity' of Iolo, or later lesser writers, striving to make it spuriously mysterious; but, even with these specific squabbles, we will find Iolo, as a phenomenon, immensely intriguing and of utmost significance in the history of the soul of Wales.

II. Proceed down A4120, and just past the Devil's Bridge itself turn sharp left on B4574 (signposted Cwmystwyth and Rhayader). At Cwmystwyth, keep left and take the mountain road to Rhayader, your last look at 'wild' Wales. Take care: the sheep are no problem, but an early morning motorist may make you jump, coming at you round a curve. Where the mountain road enters Rhayader is close to the riverside park you stopped at on entering West Wales eight days ago. A REST STOP there is probably in order.

From the town clock crossroads, leave Rhayader on A470 towards Builth Wells. Take this fast road for about ten miles, then look out for B4358 off to the right (signposted to Beulah). In about 3 miles, at Llanafan-fawr, turn left at the sign to Cilmeri. This will be your last narrow Welsh country road; enjoy the four miles to the junction with A483. The monument we are seeking is to the right about a hundred yards on A483 west, where there is a place to park on the left-hand side of the road at the entrance gate.

8.2 Cilmeri and the Monument for Llywelyn the Last (died 1282)

NEAR THIS SPOT
WAS KILLED
OUR PRINCE
LLYWELYN
1282

The present memorial was erected by the Builth Wells Rural Council in June 1956, with the gift of a granite monolith from the Caernarfon County Council.

The Cilmeri monument

We need not go into the details of Llywelyn's skirmishing and manoeuvring to become the Prince of a unified Wales; it required much unpleasant harshness as well as undoubted valour. The Treaty of Montgomery of 1267 established him at his height; but a new Edward coming in in 1272, and Llywelyn's intransigence, led to an English invasion and a reduced status for Llywelyn with the Treaty of Aberconwy 1277. After a restless few years, in a rebellion provoked by his brother Dafydd, Llywelyn marched south again in 1282. His death came near Builth; it was a rather untidy, 'melancholy' end, as J.E.Lloyd describes it:

He died, not at the head of his army in a well-fought fray, but almost alone, in an unregarded corner of the field, as he was hastening from some private errand to rejoin the troops who were holding the north bank of the Irfon against a determined English attack. The man who struck him down with his lance, one Stephen Frankton, knew not what he had done, and it was only afterwards that the body was recognized. It is probable that the true story of that fateful 11th of December will never be rightly known and, in particular, why Llywelyn, with dangers on every side, had thus allowed himself to be separated from his faithful troops.

Lloyd comes to the conclusion that deliberate treachery and ambush were unlikely, and that Llywelyn had gone into Builth to rally more support just when the English were making a move that accidentally cut him off. He sees no reason for rejecting the local tradition that the prince fell at the spot known as Cwm Llywelyn, half a mile from the nearby church of Llanganten.

(This church can be seen down by the river Chwefri as you drive east on A483 over the railway tracks.)

Bleddyn Fardd, the bard, wrote of Llywelyn at his death (trans. D.M.Lloyd):

> A strong man in the attack on a host on his border,
> The man of the green tents, the maintainer of the camp,
> Manly son of Gruffudd, most ungrasping giver of largesse
> In the splendid tradition of Nudd and Mordaf.
>
> A red-speared man, a man grief-stricken like Priam,
> A fine man as king over the proudest army,
> A man whose fame will spread easily – most generous his outlay –
> As far as the sun travels on his farthest course.
>
> It is a grievous thing that that man is destroyed, a most courtly
>   leader,
> A man bitterly mourned, the truest of kinsmen,
> A refined, wise, and upright man, the best from Anglesey
> To Caerleon, that fairest of places.
>
> Llywelyn who stood near the limits of the Taff,
> A leader of the people, lavish bestower of raiment.
> A man above them all, the greatest of soldiers,
> As far as Port Wygyr a calm eagle.

And another bard, Gruffudd ab yr Ynad Coch, was moved to write one of the greatest elegies of the Middle Ages, which reads in part:

> Poni welwch chwi hynt y gwynt a'r glaw?
> Poni welwch chwi'r deri'n ymdaraw?
> Poni welwch chwi'r môr yn merwinaw'r tir?
> Poni welwch chwi'r gwir yn ymgyweiriaw?
> Poni welwch chwi'r haul yn hwyliaw'r awyr?
> Poni welwch chwi'r sŷr wedi syrthiaw?
> Poni chredwch i Dduw, ddyniadon ynfyd?
> Poni welwch chwi'r byd wedi bydiaw?
> Och hyd atad Dduw, na ddaw môr dros dir!
> Pa beth y'n gedir i ohiriaw?
>
> See you not the rush of wind and rain?
> See you not the oaks lash each other?
> See you not the ocean scourging the shore?
> See you not the truth is portending?
> See you not the sun hurtling the sky?
> See you not that the stars have fallen?
> Have you no belief in God, foolish men?
> See you not that the world is ending?
> Ah God, that the sea would cover the land!
> What is left us that we linger?

III. From the Llywelyn memorial take A483 east through Builth Wells (Welsh name: Llanfair-ym-Muallt), where you pick up A470 south (towards Brecon). At a junction, keep left on A479 (signposted to Abergavenny). At Talgarth, take the right turn on to B4560 (signposted Llan-gors), and look for the sign indicating Coleg Trefeca on the the left-hand side of the road. Go up the short driveway to the car park.

The chapel to the left (looking very 'churchy' – as Howell Harris himself was never anything but a churchman, though evangelical) is normally open, as a museum, to the public. If closed, ask at the office in the new building, which houses the Laity Training Centre of the Presbyterian Church of Wales, with its conference facilities and small book shop.

8.3 Howell Harris (1714-1773) and the Community of Trefeca

Howell Harris, once described as 'a man on fire', was born to poor parents in the hamlet of Trefeca, but he managed to attend a grammar school and supported the family as a schoolmaster after his father died. The main events in Harris's life are spiritual events, the most significant being his process of conversion to the life of the proselytizer. After an awakening in Talgarth Church in April 1735, he was in a turmoil all that summer, and by December had given up his schoolteaching. He is quoted as saying:

> Now a strong necessity was laid upon me, that I could not rest, but must go to the utmost of my ability to exhort. I could not meet or travel with anybody, rich or poor, young or old, without speaking to them of religion and concerning their souls. Persuaded by my neighbours, I went during the festive season from house to house in our parish, and the parishes of Llan-gors and Llangasty, until persecution became too hot. I was absolutely dark and ignorant with regard to the reasons of religion, I was drawn onwards by the love I had experienced, as a blind man is led, and therefore I could not take notice of anything in my way. My food and drink was praising my God. A fire was kindled in my soul and I was clothed with power and made altogether dead to all earthly things. I could have spoken to the King were he within reach – such power and authority did I feel in my soul over every spirit –

There were various stages to the founding of the Trefeca community, including a preliminary one at Wernos Farm. But it was in 1750, after fifteen astounding years in the mission field, and in growing conflict with his great mentor Daniel Rowland, that Harris 'retired' to Trefeca to found a religious community where his followers could share the religious life together in work and worship. In a few years the 'Family', as it was called, had grown to one hundred persons, applying advanced agricultural methods in their farming. A convert and patroness, the Countess of Huntingdon, worked to provide the seminary for religious training.

Coleg Trefeca

The history of the Trefeca community after Harris's death in 1773 is a story of struggle and compromise. At this spot it is better to reflect on the life of the man who has been regarded as the foremost Welshman of his age. O.M.Edwards wrote of him: 'The awakening of Wales from a sleep that was paralysing its national vigour can be attributed to him more than anyone else.' His remains were taken, by law, to the consecrated ground of Talgarth Church. We do not seek them there. Trefeca is where his spirit is found, and where you can read a facsimile of the wording that was carved on his tombstone:

Near the Altar lie the Remains of
HOWELL HARRIS Esquire,
Born at Trevecka January the 23rd 1713/14 O.S.
Here where his Body lies, He was convinced of Sin,
Had his Pardon Sealed,
And felt the Power of Christ's precious Blood,
At the Holy Communion.
Having Tasted Grace, He resolved to declare to others

What God had done for his Soul.
He was the first itinerant Preacher of Redemption
In this Period of Revival in *England* and *Wales*.
He Preached the Gospel
For the Space of thirty-nine Years,
Till He was taken to his final rest.
He received all who fought Salvation
Into his House –
Thence sprung up the Family at
Trevecka.
To whom He faithfully Ministered unto his end,
As an indefatigable Servant of GOD,
And faithful Member of the *Church of England*.
HIS END
Was more blessed than his Beginning.
Looking to Jesus crucified
He rejoiced to the last, that Death had lost its Sting.
He fell a Sleep in Jesus at *Trevecka* July 21st 1773,
And now rests blessedly from all his labours.

IV. Proceed south on B4560 to the junction with A40, turn left and go east towards Abergavenny, but at Crickhowell take the right turn across the river Usk on A4077 to Gilwern; continue across A465 through Gofilon and look for B4246 to the right. Take this over the top to Blaenavon. Coming down the hill to the Texaco station, turn right at the sign to the 'Big Pit', and take B4248 about a mile until you see the 'Big Pit' signposted on the left. Drive to the car park.

8.4 The 'Big Pit' of Blaenavon

Pwll Mawr colliery ('Big Pit') has been successfully converted to a visitor's park, where one can experience a descent into the actual mine. Give 1½ hours if you want the full treatment, but there is much to experience without the underground tour, and for most people it will be enough to go through the surface 'mining galleries' on the way to the baths and the museum, and the cafeteria for a REST STOP.

When one realizes that, up to 1939, the men who worked these mines had to travel to and from the pit in their working clothes and wash at home, and that pit-head baths came into existence only when they had been paid for collectively, then it is clear why trade union leaders figure so importantly in the history of South Wales. We turn now to one of those leaders, one who had heroic stature in these parts, and beyond.

> **V. From the colliery to Bryn-mawr on B4248; take the road signposted to Beaufort (A4248), which joins the road signposted to Ebbw Vale, and later Tredegar (A4047 west). Eventually, as you come up a rise, you will see on the right something like a 'stonehenge' on the horizon. Make a quick right turn into the car park. (There is a sign but it is quite small.)**

8.5 The Aneurin Bevan Monument, Ebbw Vale

It was here
ANEURIN BEVAN
spoke to the people
of his constituency and the world.

Yes, his local voters and general world opinion: these made up Bevan's twin vision; and it does leave out Wales as an entity. When Gwynfor Evans said: 'Wales did not produce one socialist leader who was ready to put Wales first, let alone die for her' – he had the Irish labour leader James Connolly in mind, and he sums up Bevan with the words: 'that great but deracinated politician.'

But Aneurin Bevan gets a full page portrait in *Land of My Fathers* next to Saunders Lewis. He was brought up in the chapel and the eisteddfod; he was named after the poet Aneurin Fardd, a friend of his father's; he was a miner for a while in Tredegar; he was unemployed with the rest, until his left-wing passions became his vocation and he rose to fame because of his natural abilities in politics. Anyone who heard him speak to a working-class crowd has been blessed with something extremely rare. He was melodious and harsh, down to earth and visionary, he created humour while ridiculing enemies and joshing his friends. I imagine Lloyd George was like that; but Bevan also had a cause, the socialist brotherhood

171

of man. I heard him say those words, 'the brotherhood of man', in my local townhall square, and I shall never forget the thrill of every member of the gathering. There was something there to be proud of that one can hardly expect to see the like of again. This windy spot above the mining valleys that lifted up their hearts to Aneurin Bevan's oratory only emphasizes the loss.

> **VI.** *Continue west on A4047, which becomes A4048 as it makes its way up to the main artery A465. Go west for about five miles, ignoring the first exit to Merthyr Tydfil, and taking the A470 exit south. Follow the signs to 'City Centre'; when a long high stone wall on the left-hand side of the road gives way to a black iron gateway, this is your sudden turn into the park driveway of the castle.*

8.6 Cyfarthfa Castle Museum

One does not have to spend too long here, just long enough to get an idea of how 'the other half' lived, the mill and mine owners. It was the demand for cannon in the Napoleonic Wars which made Cyfarthfa the largest iron works in the world by the turn of the century. Nelson visited the operation in 1802. The castle was built for William Crawshay II in 1825 at the cost of £30,000. But the Crawshays were slow in converting to steel, and were taken over by competitors in 1902, and had largely left the scene by 1910. Because of the family's concerns taking them elsewhere, the museum that Cyfarthfa has now become includes original furnishings, plate, paintings, furniture, a fairly complete panorama of what it meant to be on top.

One oddity stands out: the bust of Keir Hardie, on the right as one enters. Keir Hardie (1856-1915) was a miners' leader, a founder of the Labour Party and, though from Scotland, was returned as MP for Merthyr Tydfil. 'He was an honest man of high principles,' writes Gwynfor Evans. 'Under the leadership of Keir Hardie the Labour Party identified itself with every national cause and institution in Wales.' But the ideology of the international class war came to dominate, and the hope for Labour as a national party for Wales has never returned. Hardie himself, a Christian pacifist, was crushed by the jingoism of the First World War; within a year of the outbreak of war, he was dead at 59. It is gratifying that the Cyfarthfa museum allows him a place as the noble adversary of the system that amassed such wealth into one place at widespread human cost.

> *VII. Exit and turn left and left again on to the main road. Turn immediately to the right at the sign to Cardiff. Continue on A470 through Merthyr Tydfil and on to Cardiff. You will pass the M4 motorway to England. (Some may be tempted to take it; but they will miss the capital of Wales, Cardiff, and a genius of Wales's Welshness, Iolo Morganwg.)*
>
> *Keep in the right lane as you approach Cardiff on A470, follow signs to 'City Centre', and before you know it (if you have avoided the rush hour) you will find yourself on the majestic North Road, Bute Park on your right and the University and civic buildings on your left. All traffic turns right at the Castle, and the slowness of the traffic will enable you to see the sights.*

8.7 Cardiff Centre

Merthyr Tydfil was the only large town in Wales in the first half of the 19th century. In 1851 it had a population of 63,080, while Cardiff had only 18,341. But Cardiff had a sea port, and the canal from Merthyr fed the docks, and in 1911 Cardiff had over 180,000. Its wealth made it the obvious choice for the national capital, declared in 1955. Any attentive reader of this book will feel that this was a mistake: Aberystwyth is the natural centre. As we have seen, the National Library and the University were founded in Aberystwyth. Cardiff has the National Museum, with the Folk Museum just outside at St Fagan's; but they are not part of this guide to Welsh Wales. As

Dylan Thomas once said of Swansea Museum, they should be 'in a museum'. They are not part of living Wales.

VIII. From Cardiff centre we are leaving in the direction of Rhoose Airport, west of the city beyond Barry. There are alternative routes for getting out. If you find yourself on Leckwith Road (A4055), this is the way to Barry ring road, and you will see signs to Rhoose (Cardiff) Airport. If you find yourself on Cathedral Road or Cowbridge Road, these will take you up to A48; go west, and you will see signs to Cardiff Airport. At the airport, continue straight on; A4226 becomes B4265. At St Athan, turn right, past RAF Station St Athan, and look out for the signpost to Flemingston on the right. You are soon at the village; park at the church, and ask for the key from Mr Thomas at the adjacent house to the east.

8.8 Iolo Morganwg of Flemingston

Why would one want to go so far out of one's way to pay tribute to Iolo Morganwg? The answer is that he is a very special person indeed. He single-handedly changed the direction of the aspirations of his countrymen in a massive and enduring way. This transformation, of course, would not have happened if the Welsh were not temperamentally and traditionally inclined to value scholarship, poetry, and antiquarian matters.

This is what you will read on the plaque inside Flemingston Church:

In Memory of
Edward Williams
(Iolo Morganwg)
of this village
Stonemason, Bard, and Antiquary

Born at Penon, in the adjoining Parish of Llancarfan, on the 10th day of March (Old Style) AD 1746. Died on the 18th December, 1826. His Remains are deposited near this spot.

His mind was stored with the histories and traditions of Wales. He studied Nature, too, in all her works. His mortal part was weak, and rendered him little able to ply his trade; but God endowed him with mental faculties – patience of research and vigour of intellect – which were not clouded by his humble occupation. He was never at school, yet he became a large contributor, of acknowledged authority, to bardic and historic literature. His simple manners, cheerful habits, and varied knowledge, made him a welcome visitor within the manors of the rich as well as the cottages of the poor; and many there are in Gwent and Morganwg who still have kindly recollections of him; by these, and others, who appreciate the fruits of his genius, this Tablet was erected, Annus Domini 1955.

The plaque then quotes the Poet Laureate, Robert Southey, on Iolo Morganwg:

There went with me
Iolo, old Iolo, he who knows
The virtue of all herbs of mount or vale,
Or greenwood shade, or quiet brooklet's bed,
Whatever love of science, or of song,
Sages and Bards of old have handed down.
(from *Madoc*)

Some reports have him as extremely irritable, as a single-minded champion of idiosyncratic ideas might be. But we don't have to worry about his temper now. What we have are the results of his striving. Chiefly, it is the connection he made of the Welsh bardic tradition to the even more remote Celtic druidical pantheistic power, and his assertion that the continuous flow of inspiration from earliest times has not stopped, but exists in at least one survivor, Iolo himself, and can be reactivated outward from his person through anyone who senses his or her own connectedness. Iolo proved this contention in a most dramatic fashion. He immersed himself in medieval Welsh poetic manuscripts and learnt the ways of the *cywydd* form so well by imitating Dafydd ap Gwilym that when the London Welsh asked him to find more Dafydd ap Gwilym manuscripts he sent his own poems and they were accepted as the famous poet's and included in the 1780 edition to the great pleasure and satisfaction of the editors and many thousands of readers up into the 20th century, when the facts of the case were exposed by Griffith John Williams in a scholarly study that was presented to the world not without admiration of Iolo's brilliance. The real trouble was that Iolo's son, Taliesin Williams (also buried in this churchyard, according to the plaque), was so devoted to his father that he

175

persisted in a series of posthumous publications of papers that there is no evidence Iolo meant to publish as anything other than speculation emanating from what Malkin called his 'conjectural sagacity'. The term 'forgery' has been bandied about by people who have not examined what he himself did and the spirit in which he did it. When you come right down to it, he was a creative artist with the matter of history, making it alive and usable for himself and his contemporaries, who were, given the period, very much of a romantic bent: they wanted more that the sordid present.

The Gorsedd was such an attempt to inject poetry into a humdrum world. As a self-proclaimed bard on the basis of many years of work, mainly lonely apprenticeship, Iolo organized an innovative druidical ceremony – at Primrose Hill, because he happened to be living in London at the time, and the London Welsh wanted it as a reflection of their radical bent. The Gorsedd later organized at Cardiff on top of Garth mountain was disallowed by the constabulary as possibly signalling to the French fleet; but the real objection went deeper, for the Gorsedd was essentially subversive to English authority. It claimed as of highest value something the English could never have – a continuum with the Celtic world. Iolo made up all the hymns and ceremonies; but who can deny that he was as close to being a druid as anyone ever came since 400 AD? The authenticity derived from scholarly knowledge and passion; what he presented was psychologically true. 'Truth against the World' was his slogan, now on the plaque we shall see in Cowbridge where was located the bookshop in which he sold the prohibited Thomas Paine *The Rights of Man*. I see Welsh nationalism as resting on the same sort of stubborn truth, asserted against an overwhelming imperialist force. The present day Welsh Language Society (Cymdeithas yr Iaith Gymraeg) has been as imaginative and ornery as Iolo. I once asked Language teacher Randall Isaac if he could reasonably hope to get Glamorgan speaking Welsh again. 'Yes,' he replied, 'and then we start on Hereford!' That sounds like Iolo to me, and why Iolo has rightly been called the spiritual father of modern Welsh nationalism. This is the man whose memory it is right for you to take with you out of Welsh Wales. His cottage in Flemingston no longer exists; but look around, and imagine any of those you see as somewhat smaller and stonier and grubbier, and containing a small asthmatic man, propped up in his chair through the early hours of the night, writing away, adding daily to the pile of papers which were his vision of a nation of Wales unified by its literary and sacred past, and staunch in its difference from other nations.

IX. From Flemingston, go north on the unnumbered road through St Mary Church or St Hilary – all roads north lead to A48 and Cowbridge and the opportunity for a REST STOP at numerous places on the one main street. You will find the plaque on the south side of the street on the side of a shop where Iolo Morganwg is thought to have had his bookshop, opposite the Old Town Hall.

8.9 Iolo's Plaque at Cowbridge

Those who put up this plaque in 1926 to commemorate the centenary of Iolo Morganwg's death must have had faith that future passers-by on the main street of Cowbridge would one day understand Welsh. Here is a translation of the Welsh, and the runic last line:

IN MEMORY OF

Edward Williams (Iolo Morganwg) 1747-1826, stone mason, Bard of Freedom, Antiquarian and one of the greatest benefactors of the Literature and History of Wales.

This stone was placed here by the East and Mid Glamorgan sections of the National Union of Welsh Societies, one hundred years after his death on December 17th 1826, to mark the house in which Iolo Morganwg sold books.

'TRUTH AGAINST THE WORLD'

X. Take A48 east, towards Cardiff; then take the new road A4232 north to M4; and then, if you have to leave, take the motorway over the Severn Bridge. Hwyl!

BOOKLIST

Aaron, Jane 'Daughters of Dissent' *Planet* 94 (August -September 1992)

Ackerman, John *Welsh Dylan* (Granada 1980)

Bowen, E.G. *The St David of History* (1982)

Bromwich, Rachel *Dafydd ap Gwilym: A Selection of Poems* (Penguin 1985)

Clancy, Joseph P. (trans) *Medieval Welsh Lyrics* (Macmillan 1965)

(trans) *The World of Kate Roberts* (Temple University/Wales University 1991)

Conran, Anthony (trans) *The Penguin Book of Welsh Verse* (Penguin 1967)

Davies, Hazel *O.M.Edwards* (University of Wales Press 1988)

Davies, John *History of Wales* (Penguin 1991)

Evans, Gwynfor *Land of My Fathers* (originally 1978; Y Lolfa edition 1990)

Welsh Nation Builders (Gomer Press 1988)

Fighting For Wales (Y Lolfa 1991)

Griffiths, Bruce *Saunders Lewis* (University of Wales Press 1979)

Guest, Lady Charlotte (trans) *The Mabinogion* (1906 and later editions)

Harris, John (ed) *Fury Never Leaves Us: A Miscellany of Caradoc Evans* (Poetry Wales Press 1985)

Houlder, Christopher *Wales: An Archaeological Guide* (Faber 1974)

Jones, Glyn & Rowlands, John *Profiles* (Gomer Press 1980)

Jones, Gwyn (ed) *The Oxford Book of Welsh Verse in English* (Oxford 1977)

Jones, J.Graham *The History of Wales* Pocket Guide Series (University of Wales 1990)

Lloyd, D.M. & E.M. *A Book of Wales* (Collins 1953)

Lloyd, John Edward *A History of Wales* 2 vols (Longmans 1911 and reprints)

Miall, Charles S. *Henry Richard MP* (1889)

Morgan, Derec Llwyd *Kate Roberts* (Cardiff 1991)

Sale, Richard *Owain Glyndŵr's Way* (Constable 1992)

Sandys, Oliver *Caradoc Evans* (1946)

Sorrell, Alan *Early Wales Re-Created* (National Museum of Wales 1980)

Stephens, Meic (ed) *The Oxford Companion to the Literature of Wales* (Oxford 1986)

Thomas, Gwyn *Ellis Wynne* (University of Wales 1984)

Thomas, Ned *The Welsh Extremist* (Y Lolfa 1973; reprint 1991)

Thomas, R.S. *Selected Prose* (Poetry Wales Press 1986)

Wade-Evans, A.W. et al *The Historical Basis of Welsh Nationalism* (Cardiff 1950)

Williams, Dafydd *The Story of Plaid Cymru* (1990)

Williams, Gwyn *The Land Remembers* (Futura Books 1978)

Williams, Gwyn A.*When Was Wales* (Penguin 1991)

Williams, Phil *Voice From the Valleys* (Y Lolfa 1981)

Dictionary of Welsh Biography (1959)
Poetry Wales (Sir T.H.Parry-Williams – Special Number) Vol 10 No 1
(Summer 1974)

INDEX

II. Persons, Institutions, etc.

III. Roads

B4393	3.III	
B4396	3.III	
B4401	3.V	
B4402	3.V	
B4405	4.IV	
B4406	4.VIII	
B4410	4.I	
B4416	5.IV	
B4459	6.VI	
B4501	5.VI	
B4518	1.IV	
B4560	8.III	8.IV
B4571	7.V	
B4572	2.II	
B4573	5.XIII	
B4574	8.II	
B4578	6.II	
B4580	3.IV	
B4582	7.VI	7.VII
B5103	3.VI	
M4	8.VII	8.X

Also published by Y Lolfa:

THE WELSH EXTREMIST

Essays on Welsh literature, politics and society today, with a new concluding chapter. Described by one reviewer as "probably the best and most important book on what is happening in Wales that has appeared in English".
0 86243 254 5
£5.95

THE CELTIC REVOLUTION

Peter Berresford Ellis' popular pan-Celtic primer surveying the histories and present prospects of all six Celtic nations.
0 86243 096 8
£5.95

TO DREAM OF FREEDOM

The gripping, bestselling story of MAC and the Free Wales Army—the men who, during the 1960s, challenged English rule in the first armed Welsh rebellion since the days of Owain Glyndŵr. Written by Roy Clews, it created such controversy that the police confiscated copies from our printing works to take to the Director of Public Prosecutions.
0 904864 95 2
£5.95

Why not start learning Welsh with our language tutors?

WELSH IS FUN

The bestselling introduction to spoken Welsh for adults by
Heini Gruffudd and Elwyn Ioan.
0 9500178 4 1
£2.95

WELSH IS FUN-TASTIC

The X-rated follow-up!
0 9500178 7 6
£2.95

GET BY IN WELSH

A basic phrasebook for tourists, fully decorated with
photographs.
0 904864 35 9
£1.50

WELCOME TO WELSH

A fuller, 15-part course that will give a good grounding in the
language. Includes grammar, exercises, conversations, photo-
stories and a basic dictionary.
0 86243 069 0
£5.95
Cassette also available @ £4.95.

It's Welsh!

A course by Heini Gruffudd for younger learners graphically presenting lively, colloquial Welsh.

0 86243 245 6

£4.95

Cassette also available @ £4.95.

Lazy Way to Welsh

Learn Welsh through cartoons only. Absorb basic Welsh words and phrases the really easy way!

0 86243 240 5

£4.95

We also publish an anti-guide to Wales!—

The Unofficial Guide to Wales

Colin Palfrey and Arwel Roberts have written this irreverent guide to Wales: you will never be able to read a Tourist Board one again! Full of catroons by Elwyn Ioan and photographs by Keith Morris and Aled Jenkins.

0 86243 309 6

Only £2.95!

We publish books about Welsh art, music, cookery as well as politics and laguage tutors. For a full list of books currently in print, send now for your free copy of our new full-colour Catalogue!

y Lolfa

TALYBONT
CEREDIGION
WALES
SY24 5HE
tel. (0970) 832 304
fax 832 782

When ordering by post, please add 15% for postage etc.

NOTE: trade distribution outside Wales is handled by Drake Marketing, St.Fagan's Road, Fairwater, Caerdydd (Cardiff) CF5 3AE; tel. (0222) 560 333, fax 554 909.